11+ Non-Verbal Reasoning

For the CEM test

Benchmark Test

This book contains two pull-out sections:

A **Benchmark Test** at the front
A **Parents' Guide to 11+ Non-Verbal Reasoning** at the back

Study Book

and Parents' Guide

Section Three

Find the figure in each row that is **most unlike** the other figures.

1. a b c d e (___)
2. a b c d e (___)
3. a b c d e (___)
4. a b c d e (___)

Find which one of the four squares **completes the sequence** on the left.

5. a b c d (___)
6. a b c d (___)
7. a b c d (___)
8. a b c d (___)

Work out which option is a **top-down 2D view** of the 3D figure on the left.

9. a b c d (___)
10. a b c d (___)
11. a b c d (___)
12. a b c d (___)

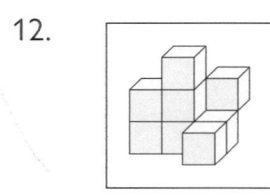

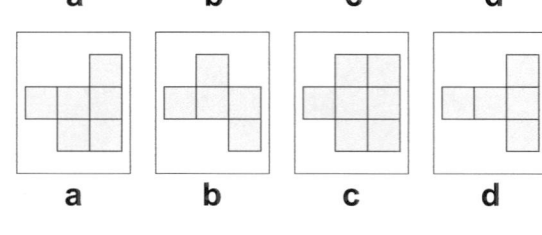

END OF TEST

/12

11+ Non-Verbal Reasoning — Benchmark Test

There are 36 questions in this test and it should take about 20 minutes. Find the answer to each question and write its letter on the line. If you get stuck on a question, move on to the next one.

Section One

Find the figure in each row that is **most unlike** the other figures.

1. (___)

2.  (___)

3.  (___)

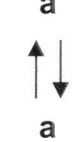

4.  (___)

Find which one of the four squares **completes the sequence** on the left.

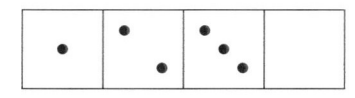

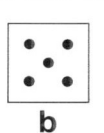

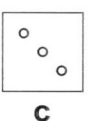

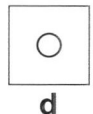

5. (___)

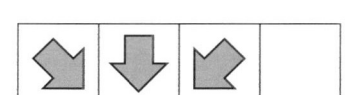

6.  (___)

7.  (___)

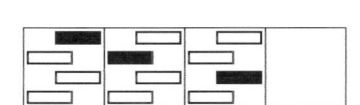

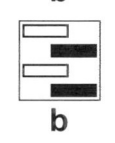

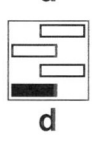

8. (___)

Find the figure on the right which is **most like** the two figures on the left.

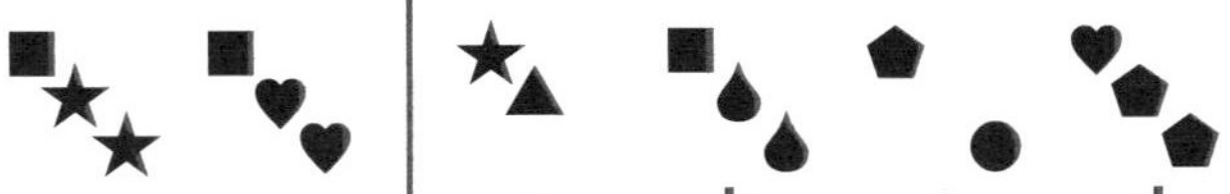

9. 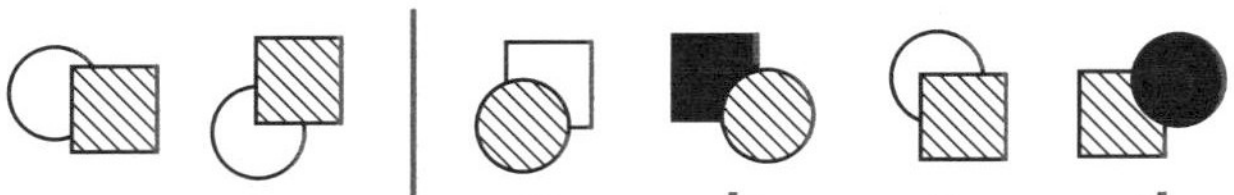 (___)

10.  (___)

11. (___)

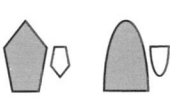

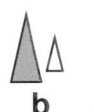

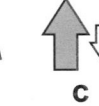

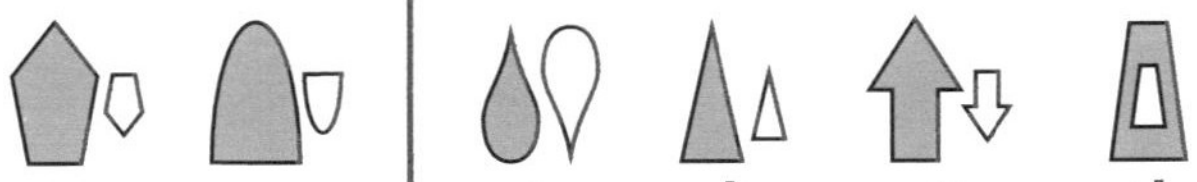

12. (___)

/12

© CGP 2018

NHRDE2

Section Two

Find which one of the four figures on the right is a rotation of the figure on the left.

1. Rotate a b c d (___)

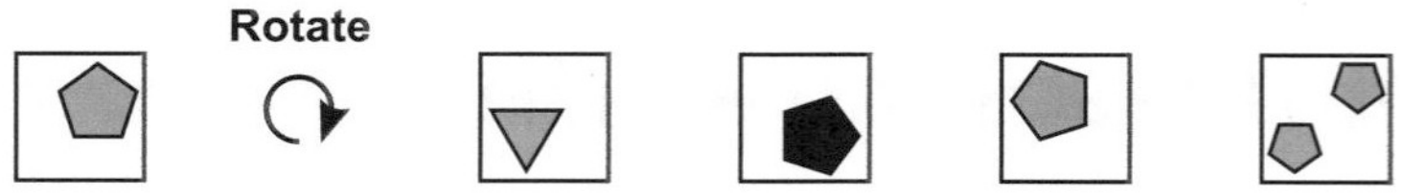

2. Rotate a b c d (___)

3. Rotate a b c d (___)

4. Rotate a b c d (___)

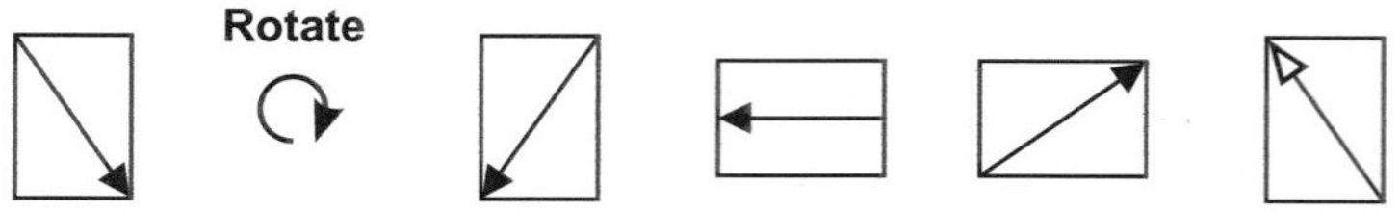

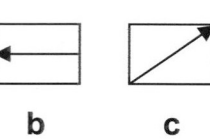

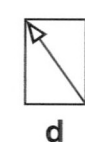

Find the figure on the right which is **most like** the three figures on the left.

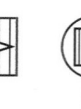

5. a b c d e (___)

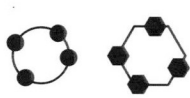

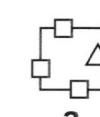

6. a b c d e (___)

7. a b c d e (___)

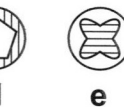

8. a b c d e (___)

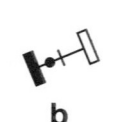

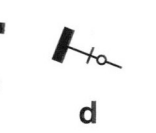

The third figure is transformed in the same way as the first. Find the figure it **transforms into**.

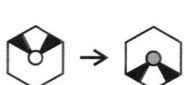

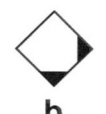

9. a b c d e (___)

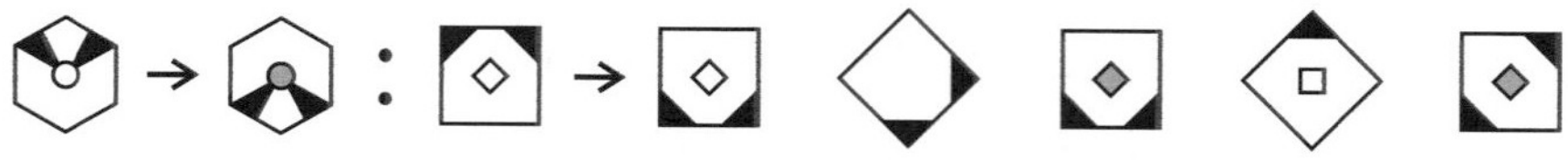

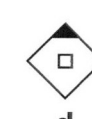

10. a b c d e (___)

11. a b c d e (___)

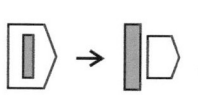

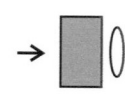

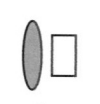

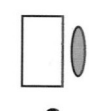

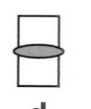

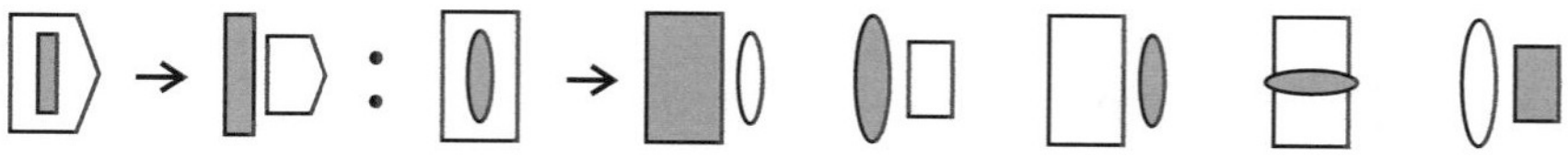

12. a b c d e (___)

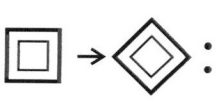

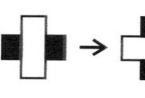

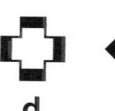

/12

© CGP 2018

NHRDE2

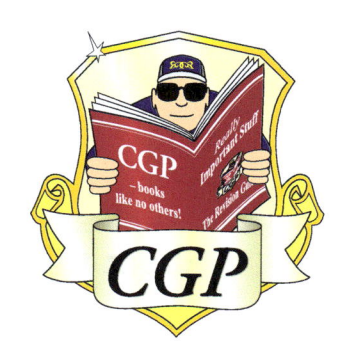

11+ Non-Verbal Reasoning

For the CEM test

Preparing for the 11+ is a tricky business, but never fear — CGP is here to explain everything children (and parents) need to know about Non-Verbal Reasoning!

We've packed this fantastic book with crystal-clear study notes, tips and examples, plus plenty of practice questions to put their skills to the test.

We've also included a helpful pull-out Parents' Guide, along with a Benchmark Test that's perfect for spotting children's strengths — and any areas they need to improve.

How to access your free Online Edition

This book includes a free Online Edition to read on your PC, Mac or tablet. You'll just need to go to **cgpbooks.co.uk/extras** and enter this code:

1784 6377 3002 9719

By the way, this code only works for one person. If somebody else has used this book before you, they might have already claimed the Online Edition.

Study Book
and Parents' Guide

Contents

About the 11+

What's in the 11+ 1
What's in the 11+ Non-Verbal Reasoning Test 2
How to Prepare for the 11+ 3

Tick off the check box for each topic as you go along.

Spotting Patterns

Spotting Patterns .... 4 ✓
Shapes .... 5 ☐
Counting .... 8 ☐
Pointing .... 10 ☐
Shading and Line Types .... 12 ☐
Position .... 15 ☐
Order .... 18 ☐
Rotation .... 20 ☐
Reflection .... 23 ☐
Layering .... 26 ☐

Question Types

Similarities and Differences

Similarities and Differences .... 29 ☐
Odd One Out .... 30 ☐
Find the Figure Like the Others .... 33 ☐

Pairs, Series and Grids

Pairs, Series and Grids .... 36 ☐
Complete the Pair .... 37 ☐
Complete the Series .... 40 ☐
Complete the Grid .... 43 ☐

Rotation and Reflection

Rotation and Reflection .... 48 ☐
Rotate the Figure .... 49 ☐
Reflect the Figure .... 51 ☐

3D Shapes and Folding

3D Shapes and Folding .... 53 ☐
3D Rotation .... 55 ☐
3D Building Blocks .... 57 ☐
2D Views of 3D Shapes .... 59 ☐
Cubes and Nets .... 61 ☐
Folding .... 63 ☐

Glossary 65
Answers 66
Index 72

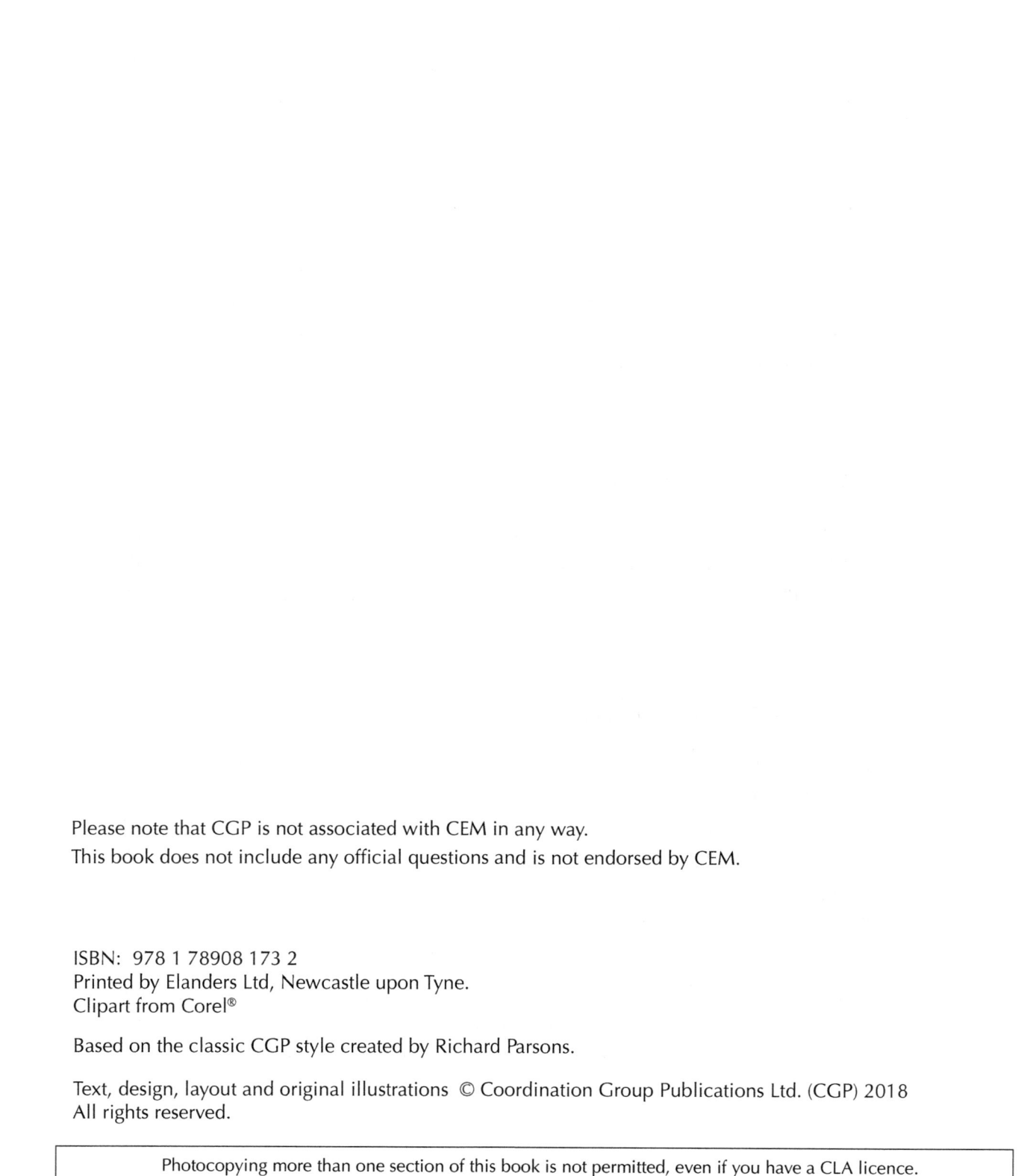

Published by CGP

Editors:
Alex Fairer and Katherine Faudemer.

With thanks to Ben Train for the proofreading.

Please note that CGP is not associated with CEM in any way.
This book does not include any official questions and is not endorsed by CEM.

ISBN: 978 1 78908 173 2
Printed by Elanders Ltd, Newcastle upon Tyne.
Clipart from Corel®

Based on the classic CGP style created by Richard Parsons.

Text, design, layout and original illustrations © Coordination Group Publications Ltd. (CGP) 2018
All rights reserved.

Photocopying more than one section of this book is not permitted, even if you have a CLA licence.
Extra copies are available from CGP with next day delivery • 0800 1712 712 • www.cgpbooks.co.uk

About the 11+

What's in the 11+

Make sure you've got your head around the basics of the 11+ before you begin.

The 11+ is an Admissions Test

1) The 11+ is a test used by some schools to help with their selection process.
2) You'll usually take it when you're in Year 6, at some point during the autumn term.
3) Schools use the results to decide who to accept. They might also use other things to help make up their mind, like information about where you live.

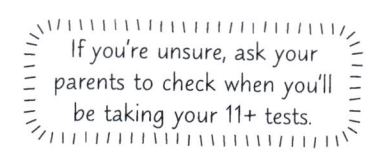

If you're unsure, ask your parents to check when you'll be taking your 11+ tests.

You'll be tested on a Mixture of Subjects

1) In your 11+, you'll be tested on these subjects:

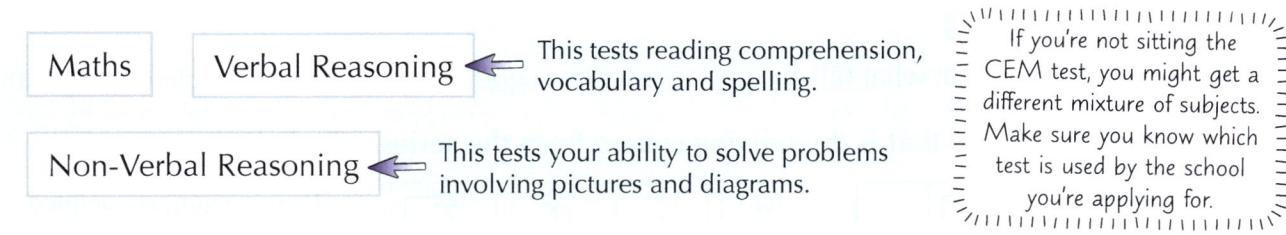

   Maths

   Verbal Reasoning ← This tests reading comprehension, vocabulary and spelling.

   Non-Verbal Reasoning ← This tests your ability to solve problems involving pictures and diagrams.

If you're not sitting the CEM test, you might get a different mixture of subjects. Make sure you know which test is used by the school you're applying for.

2) You'll probably sit two 45 minute tests, each made up of a mixture of subjects.
3) This book will help you with the Non-Verbal Reasoning part of the test.

Get to Know what Kind of Paper you're taking

Your paper will either be multiple choice or standard answer.

Multiple Choice

1) For each question you'll be given some options on a separate answer sheet.
2) You'll need to mark your answer with a clear pencil line in the box next to the option that you think is correct.

Look out for the 'Tips and Tricks' boxes in this Study Book — they'll give you practical advice about the test.

Standard Answer

1) You'll need to write down or circle the correct letter, or shade in a box under it.
2) You'll still have the same letters to choose from, though.

Check which type of question paper you'll be taking, so you know what it looks like and where your answers go. Try to do some practice tests in the same format as the test you'll be taking, so you know what to expect on the day.

# What's in the 11+ Non-Verbal Reasoning Test

Get your brain ready for Non-Verbal Reasoning by reading about the different question types.

Non-Verbal Reasoning involves Solving Problems

1) Non-Verbal Reasoning is about shapes and patterns.
2) Here are a few different question types that could crop up. We've grouped them into categories:

Similarities and Differences

You'll need to spot similarities and differences between different figures. Here's an example:

Q Find the figure that is most like the two figures on the left. Circle its letter.

They all have a black shape that's the same as the white shape, and the same way up.

Pairs, Series and Grids

You'll need to work out what fills the gap in a series, a grid or a pair of figures. Here's an example:

Q Find the figure that is the missing square from the series. Circle its letter.

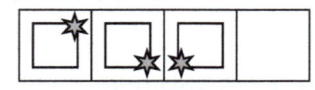

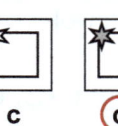

There's a grey, six-pointed star moving clockwise round the corners of the square.

Reflection and Rotation

You'll need to work out what shapes look like if they're reflected or rotated. Here's an example:

Q Work out which option would look like the figure on the left if it was rotated. Circle its letter.

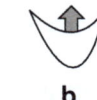

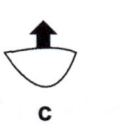

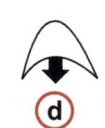

D is a 90 degree clockwise rotation. A and C are different shapes and the arrow in B is a different colour.

3D Shapes and Folding

You'll need to work out what shapes look like when they've been folded. You'll also need to rotate or combine 3D shapes, or imagine them in 2D. Here's an example:

Q Work out which option is a top-down 2D view of the 3D figure on the left. Circle its letter.

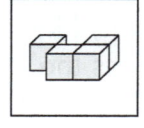

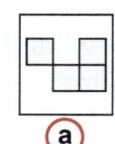

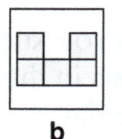

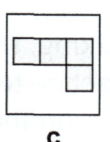

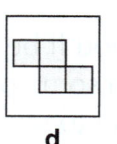

The shape has two blocks at the front of the figure and two blocks at the back with a gap between them.

About the 11+

How to Prepare for the 11+

Give yourself a head start with your Non-Verbal Reasoning preparation — be organised and plan ahead.

Divide your Preparation into Stages

1) You should find a way to prepare for the 11+ that suits you. This may depend on how much time you have before the test. Here's a good way to plan your Non-Verbal Reasoning practice:

> Do the Benchmark Test at the front of this book. Ask an adult to mark it for you.
>
> ⬇
>
> Learn strategies for answering different question types using this Study Book. Use the smiley face tick boxes at the end of each topic to record how confident you feel about tackling different question types.
>
> ⬇
>
> Do plenty of practice questions, concentrating on the question types you find tricky.
>
> ⬇
>
> Sit some practice papers to prepare you for the real test.

2) When you first start answering Non-Verbal Reasoning questions, try to solve the questions without making any mistakes, rather than working quickly.
3) Once you feel confident about the questions, then you can build up your speed.
4) You can do this by asking an adult to time you as you answer a set of questions, or by seeing how many questions you can answer in a certain amount of time, e.g. 5 minutes. You can then try to beat your time or score.
5) As you get closer to the test day, work on getting a balance between speed and accuracy — that's what you're aiming for when you sit the real test.

There are Many Ways to Practise the Skills you Need

The best way to tackle Non-Verbal Reasoning is to do lots of practice. This isn't the only thing that will help though — there are other ways you can build up the skills you need for the test:

1) Try drawing different shapes on a piece of paper. Use a small mirror to investigate what they look like when they've been reflected.
2) Copy shapes onto tracing paper to look at how different shapes change when you rotate them. This will help you to spot changes quickly.
3) Do activities like jigsaw puzzles, origami, tangrams (see p.15), draughts, sudoku and wooden or metal puzzles to help you to develop your problem-solving skills.
4) Try the warm-up activities on the pages about each question type in this Study Book. They'll introduce you to the kinds of skills you'll use to answer each type of question.

Spotting Patterns

In this section you'll be able to try your hand at all the different parts of Non-Verbal Reasoning. You need to get the hang of everything that can happen in a question if you want to do well.

What you might Have to Do

1) The best way to get good at Non-Verbal Reasoning is to do lots of questions, but first you need to know what you're looking out for. This section will help you get used to spotting the main elements of questions before you get into the details of how each question type works.
2) The real 11+ test will have questions which mix different things together. They won't be split up like they are in this section, but learning about them separately will help you understand how the real questions work.
3) If you get stuck when working through some real 11+ style questions, you can look back at this section to help you understand what's going on.

If you can't solve a question, look at the answer (but not the explanation) and try to work out why it's the right one. If you're still stuck, look at the explanation.

Questions are made up of Different Parts

This section is a good place to start if you're new to Non-Verbal Reasoning or if you want extra practice, because it deals with all the things you'll come across in full 11+ questions.

Even if you're confident about an element, you can use the practice questions for some extra practice.

Learn about and practise Each of the Elements Separately

1) Shapes — the different shapes, the importance of different numbers of sides, and symmetry.
2) Counting — when to count, what to count, and how to use basic maths.
3) Pointing — how arrows can point in directions, as well as at, or away from, an object.
4) Shading and Line Types — the different line types and shadings that a shape can have.
5) Position — where a shape is positioned in a figure.
6) Order — what an order is and how it works if the objects in an order move or change.
7) Rotation — how much an object is turned (its angle) and in what direction.
8) Reflection — when a mirror image of a shape is made by reflecting it across a mirror line.
9) Layering — how and in what ways shapes can overlap.

Some equipment will Help you Understand the Different Elements

1) As you're going through this book, you may find it helpful to have a pen, a pencil and some scrap paper. Doing a rough drawing of how you think a figure should look in questions that you're struggling with might help you work out the answer.
2) A protractor might help you see the angle and direction a figure is turned. If you have an analogue clock or watch, this might also help with clockwise and anticlockwise directions.
3) A mirror will help you understand reflection and symmetry.
4) Once you've got to grips with the basics in this book, you should put everything away apart from a pen, pencil and rough paper, as you won't be able to use the other things in the real test.

Shapes

Shapes are everywhere in Non-Verbal Reasoning. To do well, you'll need to get really good at spotting the similarities and differences between them.

Warm-Up Activity

Cut a square, a triangle and a circle out of a piece of scrap paper. See how many different ways you can fold each one in half so both sides are exactly the same.

Shapes have different Numbers of Sides

You can tell what type of shape something is by how many sides it has, so you should always count the number of sides of different shapes in a question.

Shapes of the Same Type can Look Different

1) Even though the shapes below have the same number of sides, they look different. That's because their sides are different lengths or their angles are different.

   These shapes are all triangles...   ... and these are all rectangles.

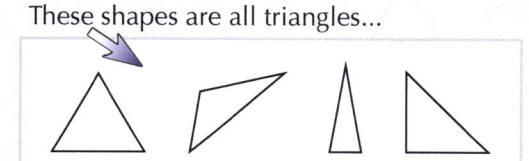

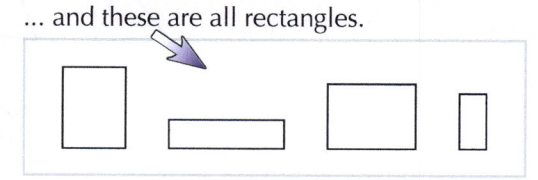

2) Some shapes will look really different, but they might still have the same number of sides.

   These are all quadrilaterals — they have four sides.   These are all hexagons — they have six sides.

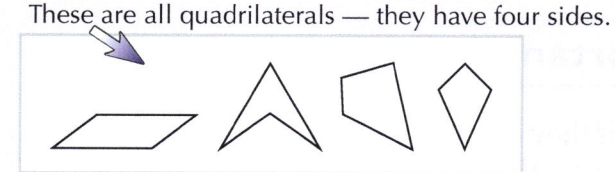

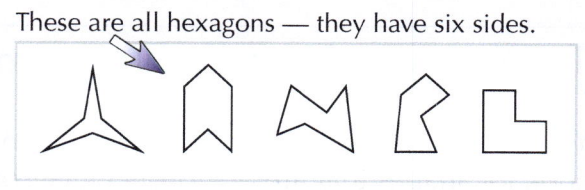

You'll need to Count the Sides of different shapes

Some questions use sequences based on the number of sides that shapes have.

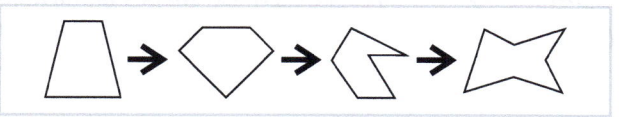

In this example, the number of sides goes up by one each time — four, five, six and seven.

Some shapes have Curved Sides

Don't forget to count curved sides as well.

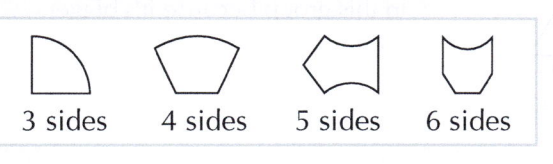

3 sides   4 sides   5 sides   6 sides

Look out for questions where you only need to look at the number of curved sides. In this example, the five-sided shape is different to the others because it's the only one with two curved sides.

Spotting Patterns

The **Sides** of a **Shape** could be **Important**

For some questions you will have to spot which shapes are similar and which are different.

Shapes might be different because they have **Different Numbers** of Sides

Sometimes you'll need to spot a shape that has a different number of sides from the rest. This can be tricky if all the shapes look very different.

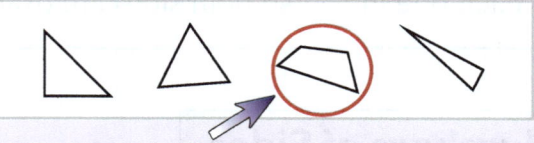

The third shape is the odd one out because it has four sides, not three.

Shapes might be different because they have **Different Lengths** of Sides

You might have to spot one different shape in a group that all have the same number of sides. Look for shapes with different angles or sides of different lengths.

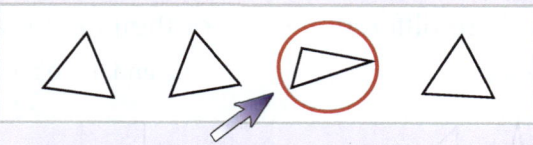

These shapes are all triangles, but the third one is different. Its sides are different lengths — the other triangles all have three sides of equal length.

The **Size** of a **Shape** could be **Important**

You can compare the size of any shapes, even if they're completely different. Look for shapes that are obviously bigger or smaller than the rest.

1) A shape might be a different size to other shapes, even though it has the same number of sides. This can be quite easy to spot if the other shapes are all the same.

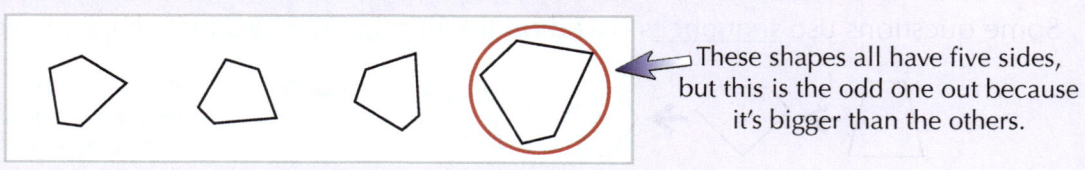

   These shapes all have five sides, but this is the odd one out because it's bigger than the others.

2) Different shapes might be the same size, even if they have different numbers of sides. When the numbers of sides are all different, they won't help you spot the odd one out — you'll need to look for another difference.

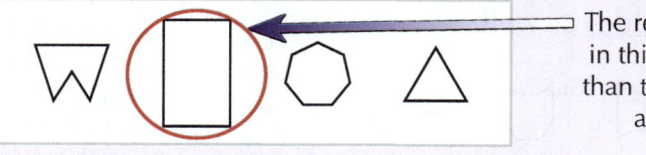

   The rectangle is the odd one out in this group because it's bigger than the other shapes, which are all about the same size.

Spotting Patterns

Some shapes are **Symmetrical**

A shape is symmetrical if you can draw a line through it that divides the shape into halves which are mirror images of each other.

1) Imagine that the shape is folded in half along a line that goes through the middle of the shape. If the two sides fit together exactly, the shape is symmetrical.

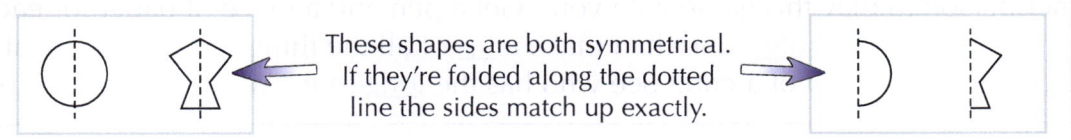

These shapes are both symmetrical. If they're folded along the dotted line the sides match up exactly.

2) If the two halves aren't exactly the same, the shape isn't symmetrical.

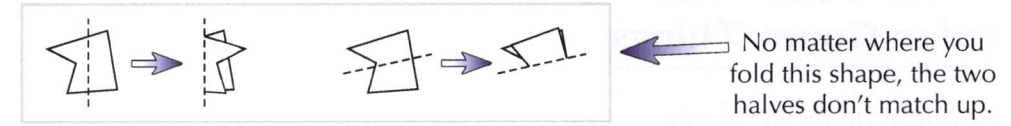

No matter where you fold this shape, the two halves don't match up.

You'll often have to think about **More Than One** shape

1) Sometimes the type of shape won't be important — you'll need to look at other things like shading, or whether its outline is solid, dotted or dashed (see p.12-14).

2) For a lot of questions, you'll have to think about other things, such as —
Do the shapes have different rotations? What is their total number of sides? How are they positioned in relation to other objects?

Practice Questions

1) Which shape is the odd one out? Circle the right letter.

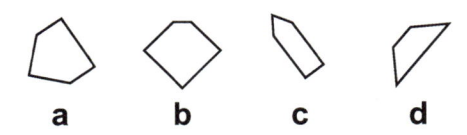

   a   b   c   d

   If any of these questions don't make sense, check out the different question types on p.30, p.33 and p.40.

2) Which shape is the most like the first two shapes? Circle the right letter.

   a   b   c   d

3) Which shape comes next in the series? Circle the right letter.

   a   b   c   d

Spotting Patterns

Counting

If in doubt, count everything — shapes, sides, dots and lines. The solution to a tricky-looking question could be as simple as how many of something there are.

Warm-Up Activity

Find another person to play this game with you. Get a pen and a piece of paper for each of you. Set a timer for two minutes, and then make a list of all the things you can see that are circles, e.g. a coin or the top of a cup. See who has the longest list when the time is up.

You'll Often need to Count Things

In easier questions it might be as simple as counting to four.

1) For some figures it will be obvious what you should count.

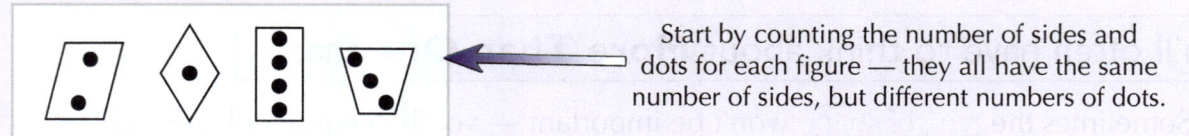

   Start by counting the number of sides and dots for each figure — they all have the same number of sides, but different numbers of dots.

2) For others it will be less obvious what you should count.

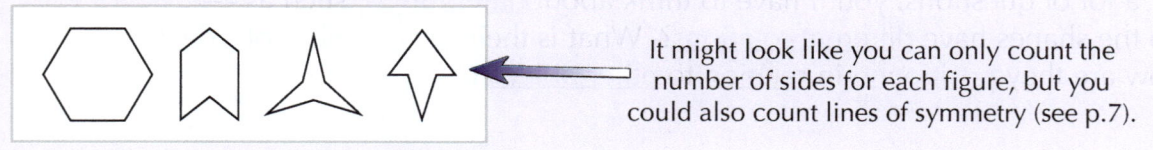

   It might look like you can only count the number of sides for each figure, but you could also count lines of symmetry (see p.7).

You might have to Add or Subtract

If there is more than one type of object, you sometimes have to do more than just count each one.

1) For harder questions you'll need to do some basic maths to work out how two numbers relate to each other. Look for relationships between the different things you can count.

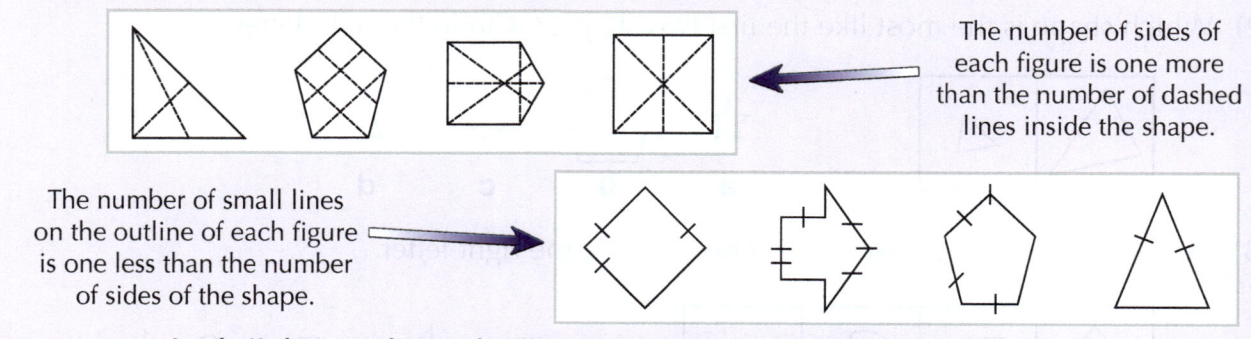

   The number of sides of each figure is one more than the number of dashed lines inside the shape.

   The number of small lines on the outline of each figure is one less than the number of sides of the shape.

2) Keep track of all the numbers of different elements in each figure. You'll find the answer to some questions by noticing that there is a pattern in the difference between two of these numbers, or in their total when added together.

Spotting Patterns

Equal Numbers of Different Objects could be Important

Add different elements together to see if their total is equal to the number of another element.

If you're looking for connections between figures, try every counting combination.

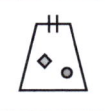

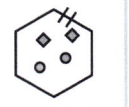

For these figures, you could count circles, squares, sides and lines (among other things).

In all these figures the number of lines added to the number of small shapes is the same as the number of sides of the large shape.

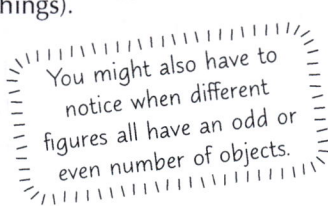

You might also have to notice when different figures all have an odd or even number of objects.

Counting is Important in Series Questions

You will often have to add or subtract for series questions.

Counting will tell you how many of each thing are added or subtracted, so you can work out what should come next.

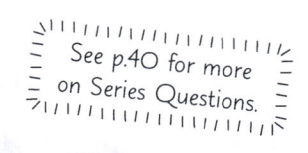

See p.40 for more on Series Questions.

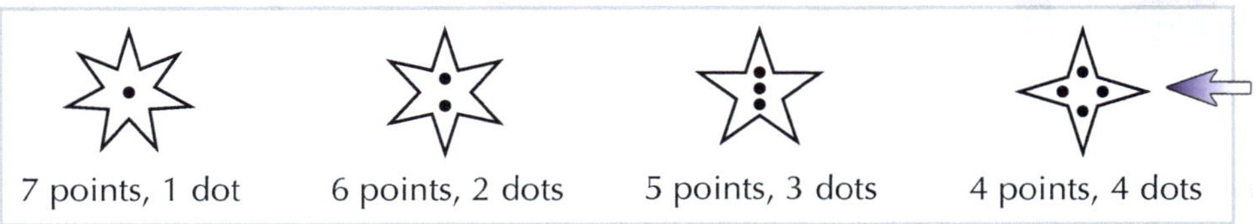

7 points, 1 dot   6 points, 2 dots   5 points, 3 dots   4 points, 4 dots

The star is losing a point in each figure, but gaining a dot. The next figure will have three points and five dots.

Practice Questions

1) Which figure is the odd one out? Circle the right letter.

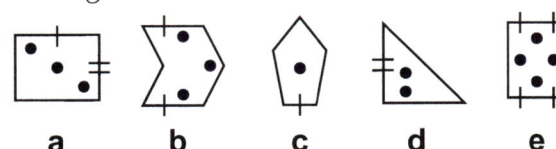

   a   b   c   d   e

2) Which figure is the most like the first two figures? Circle the right letter.

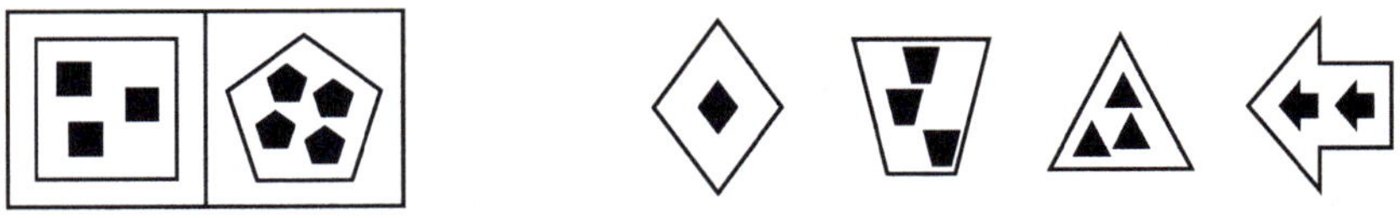

   a   b   c   d

3) Which figure comes next in the series? Circle the right letter.

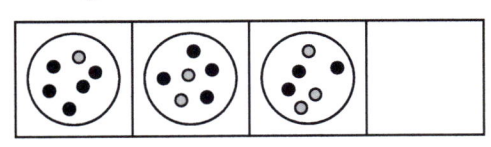

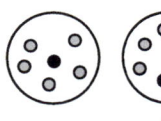

   a   b   c   d

Spotting Patterns

Pointing

Don't just look at what arrows are pointing at — it might also be important what an arrow is pointing away from, or what direction it's pointing in.

Warm-Up Activity

Cut a circle and an arrow out of card. Using a pen, divide the circle into six equal sections, and number them from one to six. Make a hole in the middle of the circle and the arrow, then use a split pin to attach them together. Try using your spinner instead of a dice in a board game.

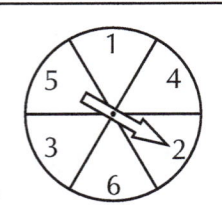

Arrows Point in a Direction

Arrows can point up, down, left and right, as well as diagonally, so you need to look at the exact direction an arrow is pointing.

1) It helps to know the different directions that an arrow can point.

   Left   Up   Right   Down

   Diagonally up... to the left. ... to the right.

   Diagonally down... to the left. ... to the right.

2) You need to notice when arrows point in the same direction or a different direction.

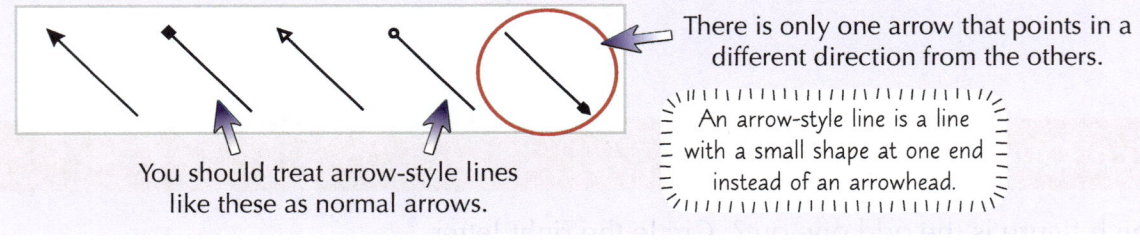

   There is only one arrow that points in a different direction from the others.

   You should treat arrow-style lines like these as normal arrows.

   An arrow-style line is a line with a small shape at one end instead of an arrowhead.

Arrows can Point At Objects

As well as direction, you should also check if an arrow is pointing towards or away from something.

1) You need to look at what an arrow is pointing at.

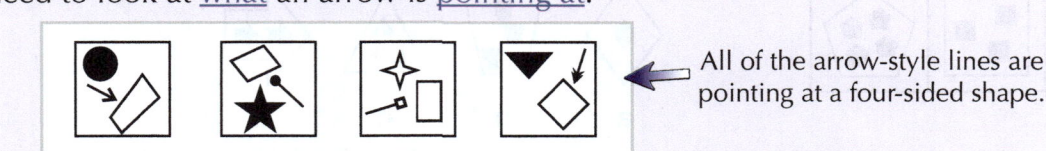

   All of the arrow-style lines are pointing at a four-sided shape.

2) It may also be important to look at what an arrow is pointing away from.

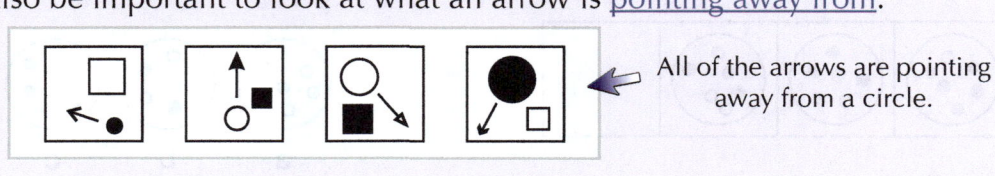

   All of the arrows are pointing away from a circle.

Spotting Patterns

Arrows can point Clockwise or Anticlockwise

Not all arrows just point in a straight line — some arrows also go in a circular direction.

1) Clockwise means the direction in which the hands on a clock move. Anticlockwise means the opposite direction.

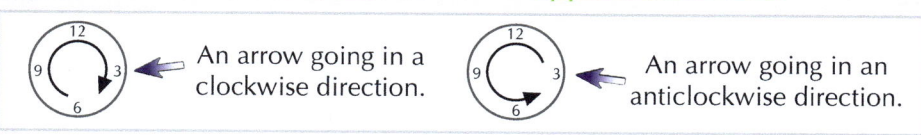

   An arrow going in a clockwise direction.   An arrow going in an anticlockwise direction.

2) All these arrows point in a clockwise direction.

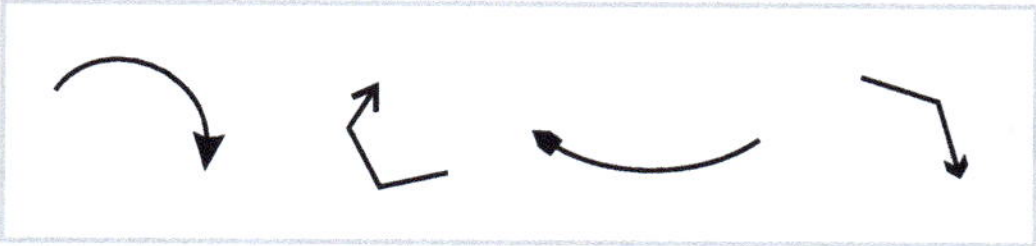

   Both straight arrows with corners and curved arrows can point in a clockwise or anticlockwise direction.

3) All these arrows point in an anticlockwise direction.

   It might help you work out if an arrow is going clockwise or anticlockwise if you imagine it going round an invisible clock face.

4) Arrows next to shapes can also suggest a clockwise or anticlockwise direction.

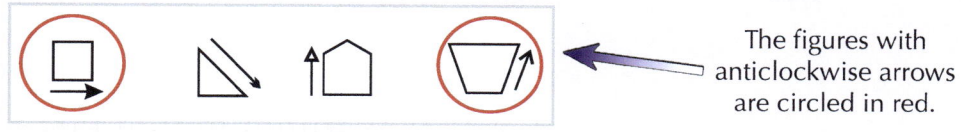

   The figures with anticlockwise arrows are circled in red.

Practice Questions

1) Which figure is the odd one out? Circle the right letter.

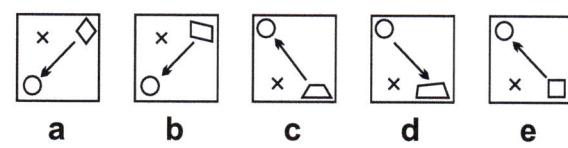

   a   b   c   d   e

2) Which arrow comes next in the series? Circle the right letter.

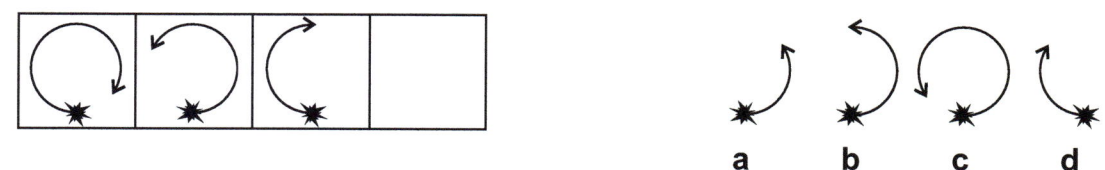

   a   b   c   d

3) Which arrow is the most like the first two arrows? Circle the right letter.

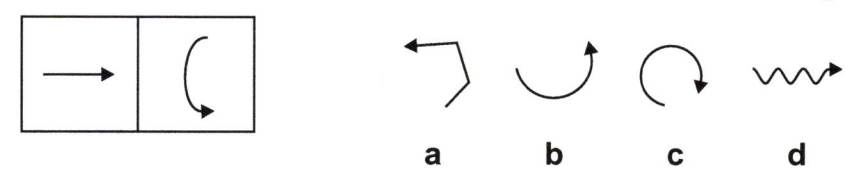

   a   b   c   d

Spotting Patterns

Shading and Line Types

Every shape that you come across will be drawn with a particular type of line, and shaded in a particular way. Recognising different line types and shadings will be an important skill for the test.

Warm-Up Activity

Draw a scribble pattern on a piece of paper using one continuous line. Using as few coloured pencils as possible, colour each shape in your scribble pattern so that no two shapes with touching sides (corners are okay) share the same shading.

It's possible to colour in all scribble patterns like this using only four colours.

Shapes can be Shaded in Different Ways

There are a few main ways that shapes are shaded.

There are other weird shadings that sometimes appear. If you come across any, don't be put off — treat them like any other type of shading.

Look out for the most common types:

| White | Black | Grey | Hatched | Spotted |

There are Different Types of Hatching

Hatching is when shapes are shaded with lines.

It's not always enough to notice that a shape is hatched — you also need to look at how it is hatched.

Check the Direction of the Hatching

It's easy to miss different types of hatching unless you check each hatched shape carefully.

These shapes are all hatched in different directions.

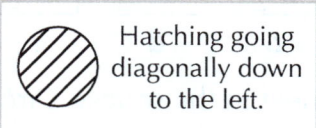

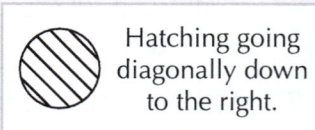

- Vertical hatching
- Horizontal hatching
- Hatching going diagonally down to the left.
- Hatching going diagonally down to the right.

Look out for Unusual Hatching

You might get a shape that is hatched in an unusual way — just treat it like any other hatched shape.

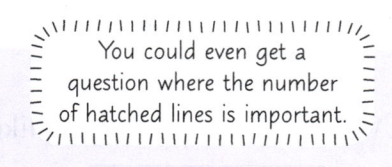

You could even get a question where the number of hatched lines is important.

These shapes are also hatched, but with different types of hatching. ➡ Cross-hatched, Thick hatching, White hatching on a black shape

Spotting Patterns

Different Shapes might share the Same Shading

When there are lots of shaded shapes, you could look for shapes that are shaded the same.

1) If the answer to a question is about the shading of large shapes it might be obvious.

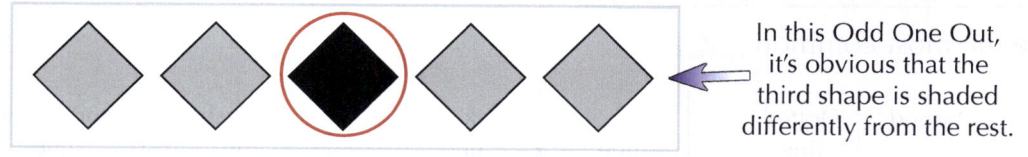

In this Odd One Out, it's obvious that the third shape is shaded differently from the rest.

2) If the answer to a question focuses on the shading of more than one shape, or a smaller part of a figure, it might be trickier to spot.

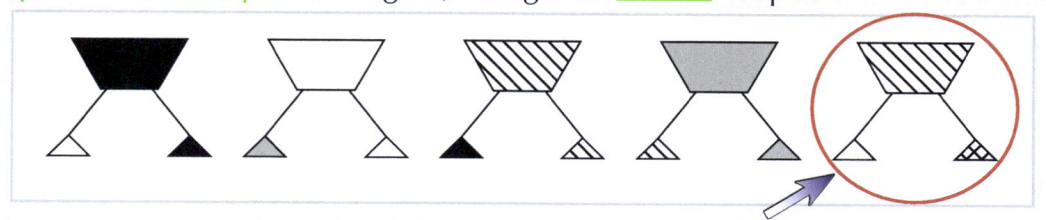

This Odd One Out is quite tricky, but by checking all the shapes and comparing them, you can work out the answer. The fifth figure is the only one with a small right-hand shape shaded differently from the large shape.

The Amount a Shape is Shaded could be Important

Different parts of shapes can be shaded, but the total amount of shading might be the same. You might need to work out what fraction of a shape is shaded.

1) Sometimes you will need to use basic maths to work out how much is shaded.

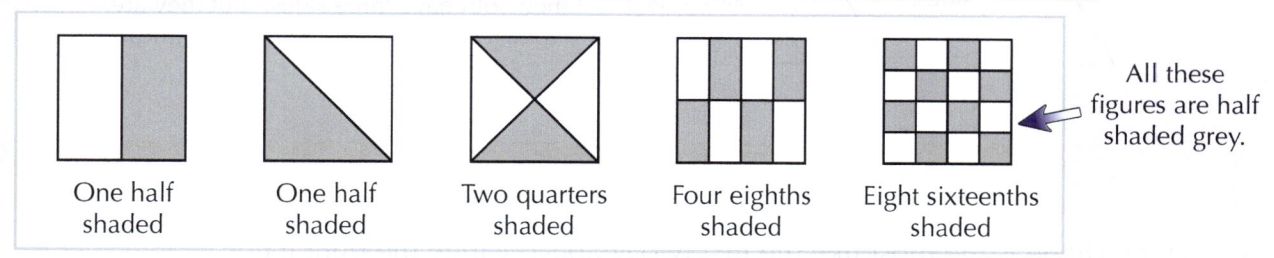

One half shaded   One half shaded   Two quarters shaded   Four eighths shaded   Eight sixteenths shaded

All these figures are half shaded grey.

2) You might have to add two different amounts of shading together.

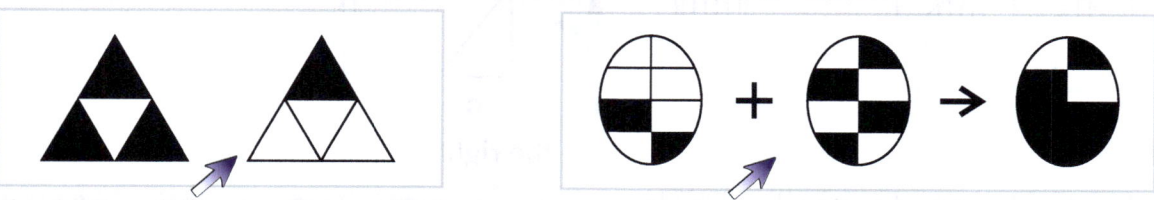

The shading of these two figures added together equals one whole shape.

The shading of these two figures added together equals three quarters of a whole shape.

3) You might have to work out how much shading needs to be added or taken away from a figure.

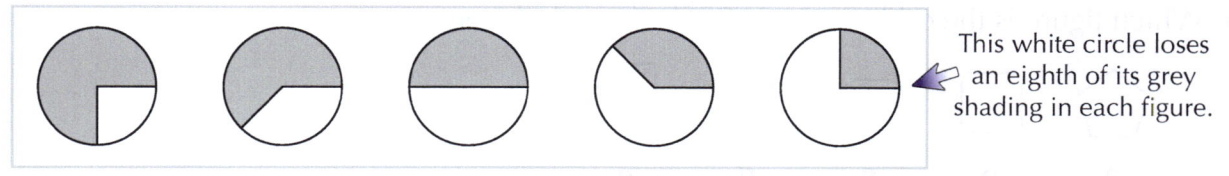

This white circle loses an eighth of its grey shading in each figure.

Spotting Patterns

Lines can be Drawn Differently

The lines of figures, arrows and the outlines on shapes can be different line types and styles. You don't need to remember them, but you need to be able to spot which lines are different in a question.

Check for Different Line Types and Styles

1) These are the most common line types.

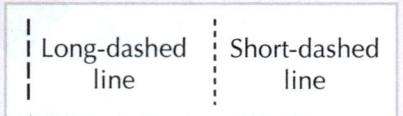

| Solid line | Dashed line | Dotted line | Thin solid line | Thick solid line | Long-dashed line | Short-dashed line |

2) Lines also come in different styles.

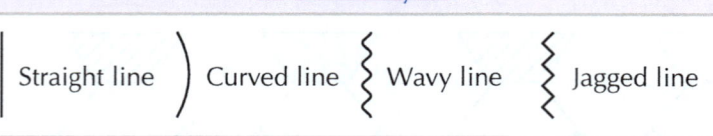

| Straight line | Curved line | Wavy line | Jagged line |

Other line thicknesses and lengths of line dashes might come up, but you only need to be able to spot the differences between different lines.

3) You'll see all sorts of combinations of line types and styles.

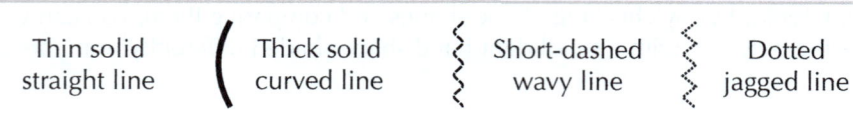

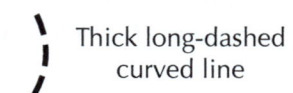

| Thin solid straight line | Thick solid curved line | Short-dashed wavy line | Dotted jagged line | Thick long-dashed curved line |

Watch out for shapes with Different Lengths of Dashes in their Outline

The number of lines used to draw a shape isn't always the same as its number of sides.

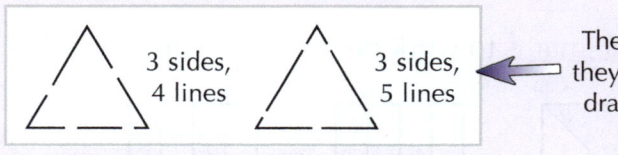

3 sides, 4 lines   3 sides, 5 lines

These two shapes are both triangles — they both have three sides. But they are drawn with different numbers of lines.

Practice Questions

1) Which shape is the most like the first two shapes? Circle the right letter.

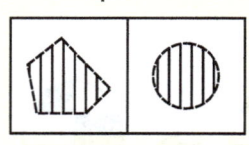

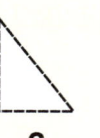

    a   b   c   d

2) Which figure comes next in the series? Circle the right letter.

    a   b   c   d

3) Which figure is the odd one out? Circle the right letter.

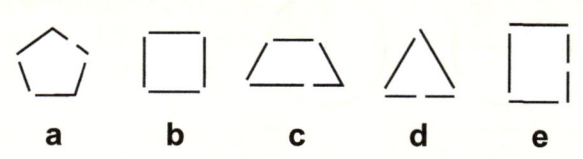

    a   b   c   d   e

Spotting Patterns

Position

Position is all about where something is — whether an object is at the top, the bottom, the left or the right of a figure — and it could be important in working out the answer to a question.

Warm-Up Activity

Trace over the shapes on the right and draw them on a new piece of paper. Position the shapes together to make different shapes. Can you use all of the shapes and make them into one complete square?

This is called a tangram.

Every Object has a Position

Noticing <u>where</u> something is sounds <u>simple</u>, but it's easy to <u>miss something obvious</u>.

Objects can have <u>similar</u> or <u>different positions</u>. <u>Keeping track</u> of <u>each shape's position</u> helps you <u>spot similarities</u> and <u>differences</u>.

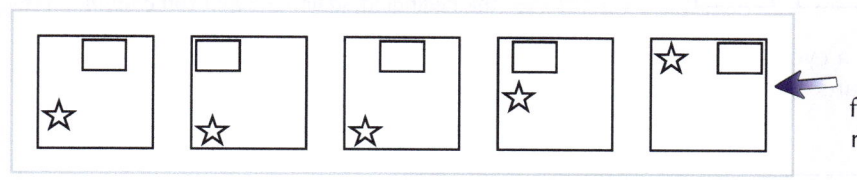

Taken together, the position of both the rectangle and the star is not the same in any of these figures, but in all of the figures the rectangle is always at the top, and the star is always on the left.

Objects also have a Position in Relation to Other Objects

When there's <u>more</u> than <u>one shape</u>, each object has a <u>position</u> other than just its <u>own</u>.

1) Two <u>objects</u> may be in <u>different positions</u> in different figures, but in the same position in <u>relation</u> to <u>each other</u>.

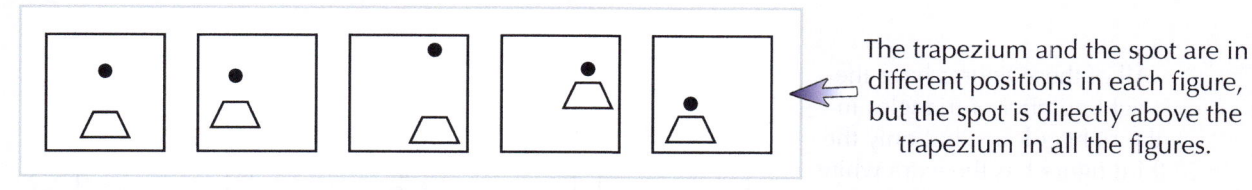

The trapezium and the spot are in different positions in each figure, but the spot is directly above the trapezium in all the figures.

2) In harder questions where there are <u>more than two</u> objects, you will need to look at the position of <u>each object</u> in relation to <u>all</u> the <u>other objects</u>.

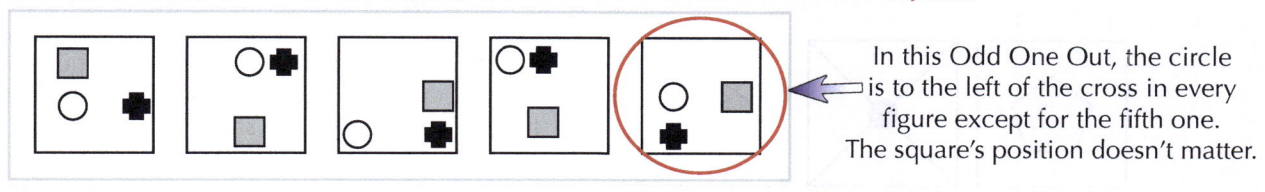

In this Odd One Out, the circle is to the left of the cross in every figure except for the fifth one. The square's position doesn't matter.

Spotting Patterns

Objects can **Move Position** in a **Sequence**

You might have to work out how an object is moving so you can decide where it should be next. Some object movements are more common than others.

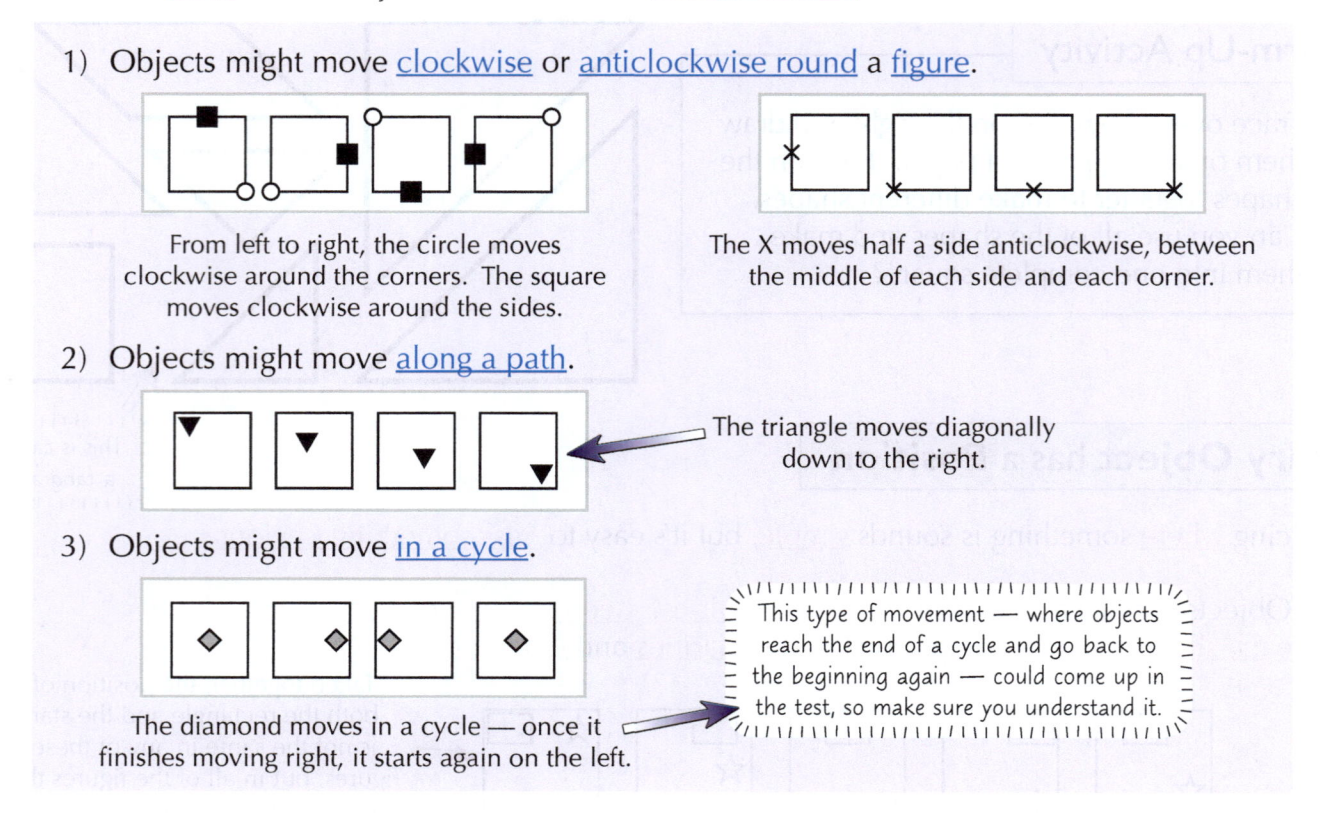

1) Objects might move clockwise or anticlockwise round a figure.

From left to right, the circle moves clockwise around the corners. The square moves clockwise around the sides.

The X moves half a side anticlockwise, between the middle of each side and each corner.

2) Objects might move along a path.

The triangle moves diagonally down to the right.

3) Objects might move in a cycle.

The diamond moves in a cycle — once it finishes moving right, it starts again on the left.

This type of movement — where objects reach the end of a cycle and go back to the beginning again — could come up in the test, so make sure you understand it.

The **Position** of **New Objects** is **Important**

When an object is added to a figure you need to look at where the new object is positioned.

1) Once you've worked out what is being added, you need to work out where it is added.

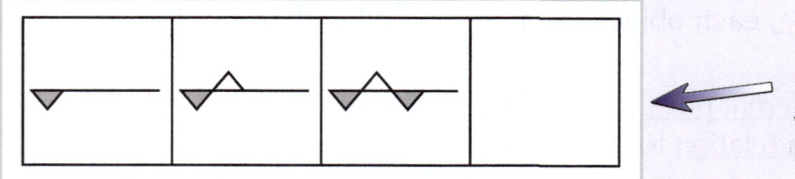

In this Series question, grey triangles and white triangles are added in turn. The missing square must have an extra white triangle, and it must be above the line on the right-hand side of the figure.

All of these figures have the right number of triangles in the right colours, but only the third figure has the extra white triangle in the correct position.

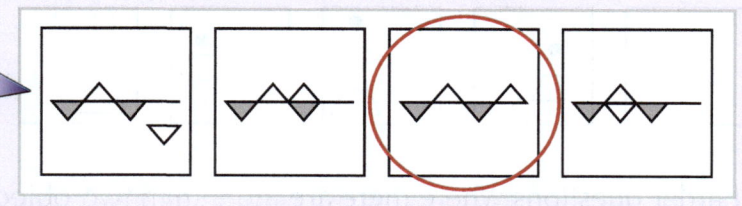

2) In some questions, two or more figures are added together to make a third figure.

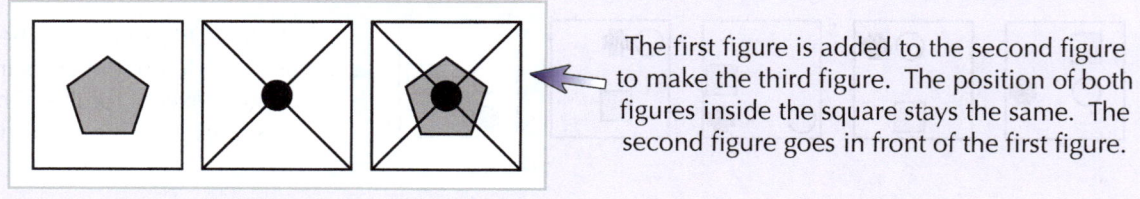

The first figure is added to the second figure to make the third figure. The position of both figures inside the square stays the same. The second figure goes in front of the first figure.

Spotting Patterns

The **Position** of objects that are **Removed** can be **Important**

It's not enough to notice when something is removed — you need to notice where it's removed from.

1) Objects or parts of an object can be removed in different ways and from different positions.

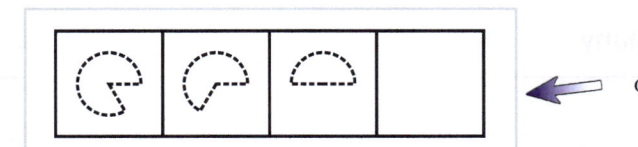

In this Series question the circle loses a sixth each time, so the next square must have a circle fraction of two sixths. The circle always loses the sixth going in a clockwise direction, so the next sixth must be removed from the left-hand side of the semicircle.

All these figures have the correct circle fraction, but only the fourth figure has it in the correct position.

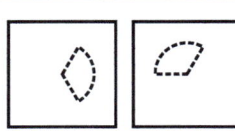

2) Even if two figures are not the same, you can see what objects should be removed by looking at their positions.

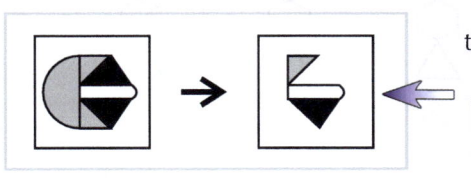

For both of these pairs, to get from the first figure to the second remove the top black shape, the bottom grey shape and the left-hand shape.

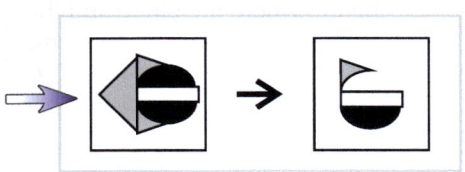

Practice Questions

1) Which figure comes next in the series? Circle the right letter.

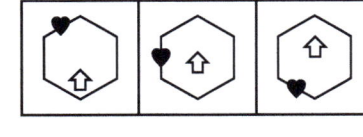

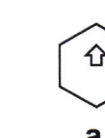

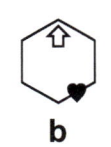

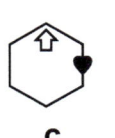

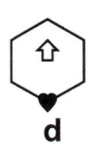

2) Which figure is the odd one out? Circle the right letter.

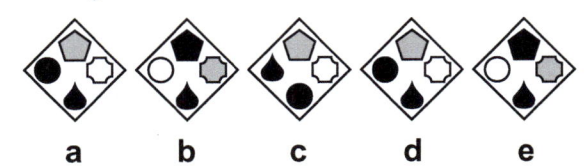

3) Which figure comes next in the series? Circle the right letter.

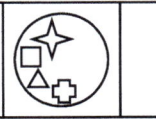

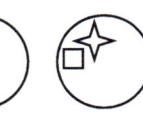

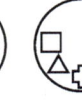

Spotting Patterns

Order

When you arrange two or more objects into a group or line, you've put them in an order.

Warm-Up Activity

Find three different coins and see how many different orders you can line them up in.

Objects can be Arranged in a Particular Order

Any group of shapes in a line can be seen as having an order.

You might have to spot whether orders of shapes are the same or different.

All these figures are in the same order except for the circled figure, where the circle and the hexagon have swapped places.

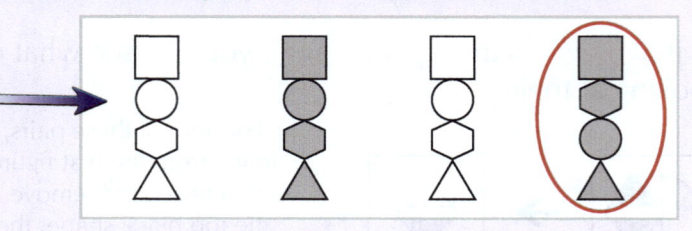

Some orders are the Same but Look Different

Shapes don't have to be in the same positions to be in the same order.

Choose a Starting Point to Check an order

1) You can check if an order is the same by starting with the same object and then counting the rest of the objects in turn.

All these figures go from left to right in the order: triangle, diamond, pentagon, except for the circled figure.

2) When you reach the end of a line of shapes (in this case the right) you should continue from the other end (in this case the left), until you have gone through every shape.

Objects can move but keep the same order. You might have to work out how each object is moving.

If an Order Moves check What Happens to the End Object

1) If all the objects in a line of shapes move positions in the same way, the end object moves to the beginning of the order.

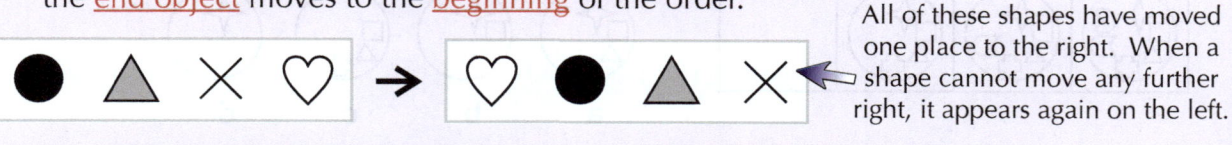

All of these shapes have moved one place to the right. When a shape cannot move any further right, it appears again on the left.

2) The movement means the order starts with a different shape. If the objects moved another place to the right they'd be arranged: X shape, heart, circle, triangle (from left to right).

Spotting Patterns

Objects can be Ordered Around a Shape

Objects round a shape might have a clockwise or an anticlockwise arrangement.

1) Pick a starting point and work round the shape in the same direction to check the order.

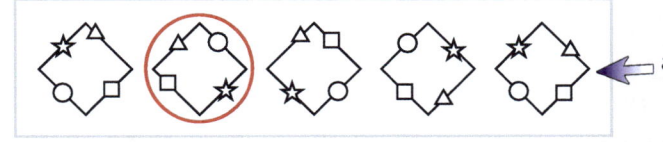

In this Odd One Out the shapes in the second figure are arranged in a different order from the rest. It goes circle, star, square, triangle in a clockwise direction. (The rest go circle, star, triangle, square.)

2) Different figures can have the same circular order but they might look different.

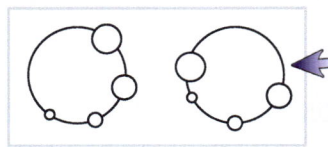

These two figures have the same order. The circles are in size order, from biggest to smallest, going in a clockwise direction.

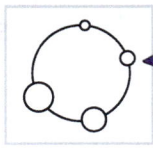

This figure looks similar, but it's arranged in size order, from biggest to smallest, going in an anticlockwise direction.

There might be More Than One Order in a question

If there is more than one order, and each order moves about, it can be hard to spot what's going on.

1) Shading is often used as a separate order, for example:

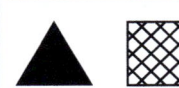

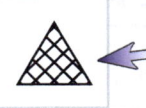

The order stays the same for both shading and shapes, but the orders have moved.

2) To work out how the two orders move you can separate them.

All the shapes move one place to the left. It goes from triangle, square, circle to square, circle, triangle.

All the shadings move one place to the right. It goes from black, cross-hatched, hatched to hatched, black, cross-hatched.

Practice Questions

1) Which figure is the odd one out? Circle the right letter.

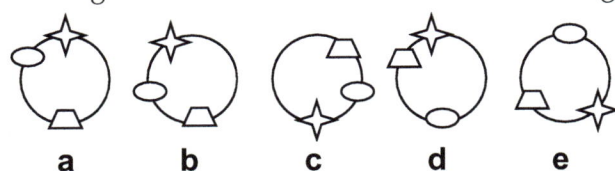

    a   b   c   d   e

2) Which figure comes next in the series? Circle the right letter.

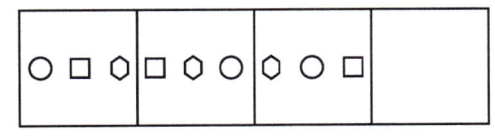

    a   b   c   d

Spotting Patterns

Rotation

Rotation is when an object is turned, either around its own centre, or around another point.

Warm-Up Activity

Draw a picture on a piece of paper. Without turning the page, try drawing how you think the picture would look upside down on a separate piece of paper. Turn the original piece of paper round to see how close you got.

Rotation is when a Shape is Turned

An object can be turned in different ways, and it will often look different after it has been rotated.

Different rotations of a shape look different from each other.

This is the same shape rotated six times. Each figure looks different because it's rotated a different amount (or angle).

Shapes can rotate Different Amounts and in Different Directions

Objects can rotate in a clockwise or anticlockwise direction.

See p.11 for more on clockwise and anticlockwise directions.

There are lots of Different Angles

1) You'll need to recognise these angles of rotation, and work out the correct direction.

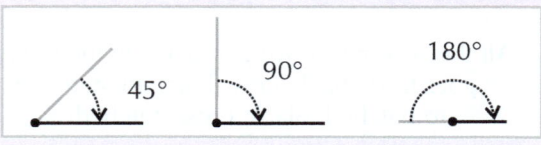

   45°   90°   180°   Clockwise   Anticlockwise

2) Knowing about angles will help you work out how much a shape is rotated.

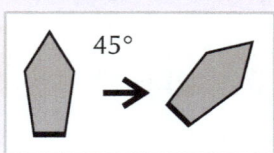

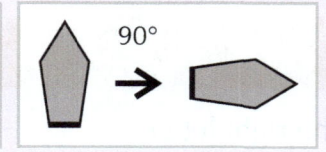

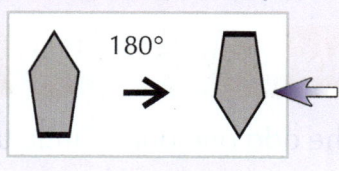

   45°   90°   180°

   The shape is rotated clockwise in each example.

Series Questions often use Rotation

Some shapes look the same when they are rotated 180 degrees — for example the first and fifth figures.

This shows how shapes might rotate in a series question.

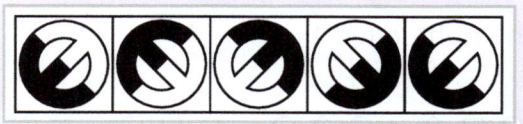

This figure is rotated 90 degrees clockwise each time.

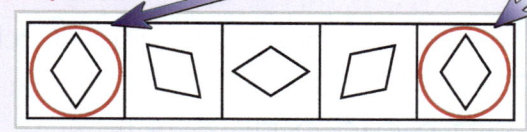

This figure is rotated 45 degrees anticlockwise each time.

Spotting Patterns

Rotation **Disguises** whether shapes are the **Same** or **Different**

Rotation can make shapes look different, even when they are the same.

It can be even harder to see whether a complicated shape has been rotated.

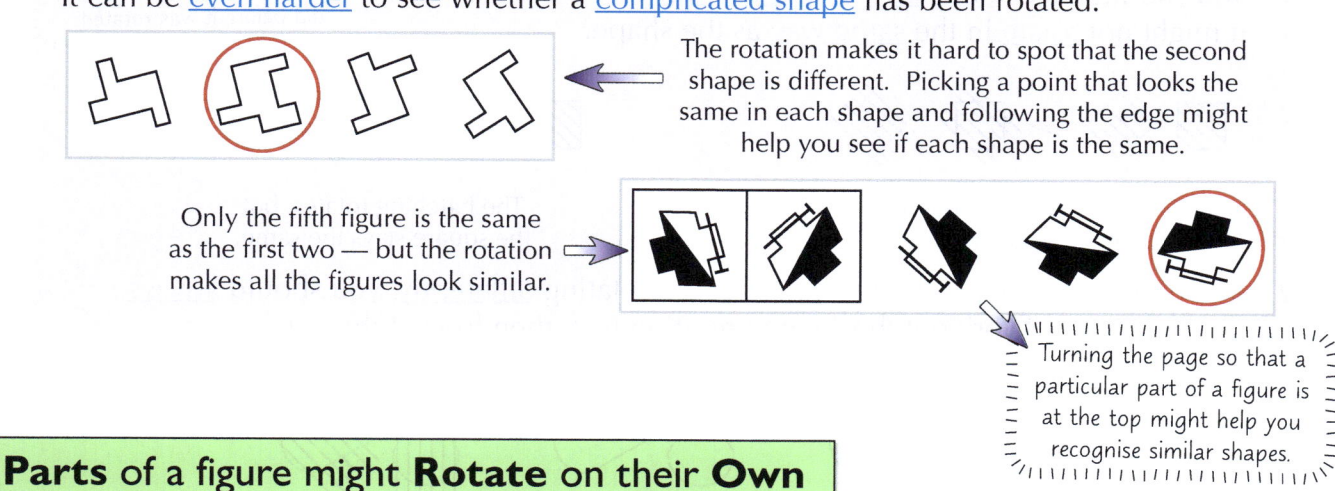

The rotation makes it hard to spot that the second shape is different. Picking a point that looks the same in each shape and following the edge might help you see if each shape is the same.

Only the fifth figure is the same as the first two — but the rotation makes all the figures look similar.

Turning the page so that a particular part of a figure is at the top might help you recognise similar shapes.

Parts of a figure might **Rotate** on their **Own**

The different parts of a figure don't have to rotate together — a part might rotate on its own, or in a different way to the rest of the figure.

1) In a complicated figure, only a small part might rotate (often other things will be happening).

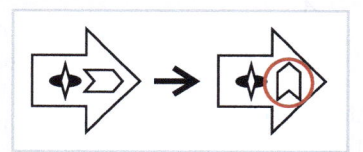

Only the small white arrowhead is rotated — the rest of the figure stays the same.

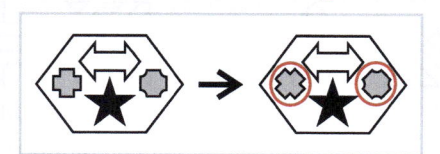

Only the small grey shapes are rotated — the rest of the figure stays the same.

2) Sometimes part of a figure will rotate round another part of the figure.

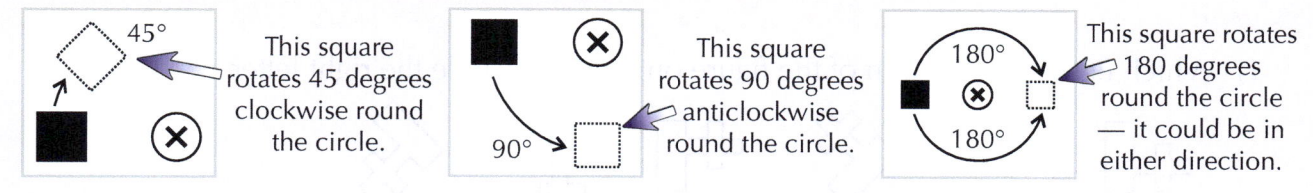

This square rotates 45 degrees clockwise round the circle.

This square rotates 90 degrees anticlockwise round the circle.

This square rotates 180 degrees round the circle — it could be in either direction.

Different Objects might **Rotate Differently**

In harder questions, you need to check the rotation of each object separately.

If you assume that everything is rotating in the same way you could make a mistake.

The black shape rotates 45 degrees anticlockwise each time.

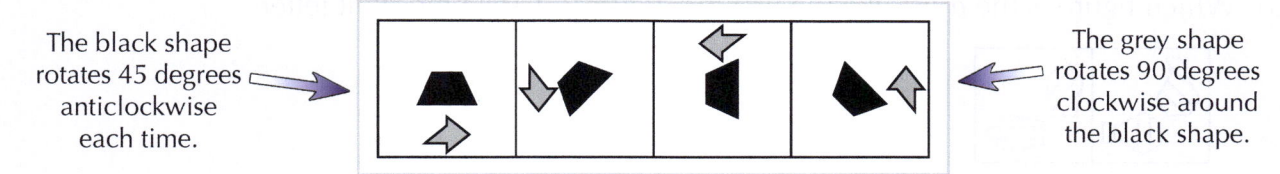

The grey shape rotates 90 degrees clockwise around the black shape.

Spotting Patterns

Hatched Shapes have Complicated rotations

Because hatching is made up of angled lines it can also be rotated.

1) You should check hatched shading carefully, because it might not rotate in the same way as the shape.

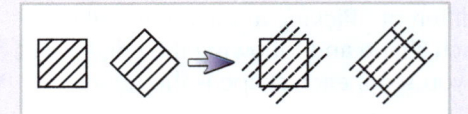

Hatching that is rotated 180 degrees looks the same as it did before it was rotated.

The square rotates, but the hatching stays the same.

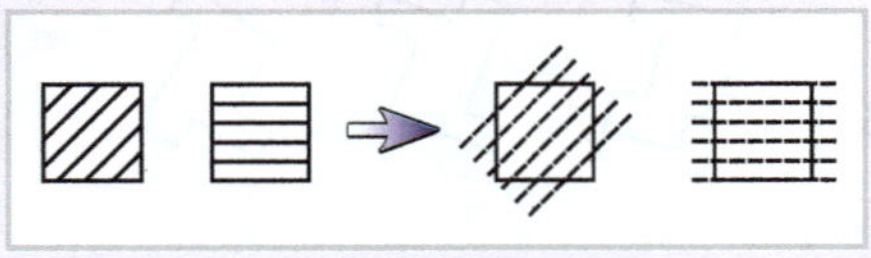

The hatching rotates, but the square stays the same.

2) If you think the shape and the hatching are rotating differently, you should always double-check. Work out the shape's rotation first, then look at the hatching.

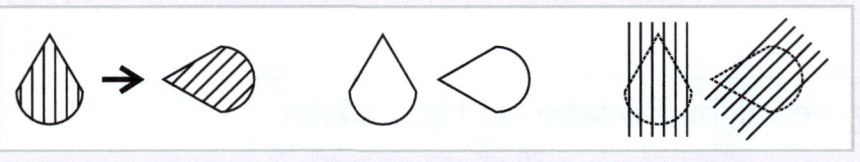

There are two rotations here.

The shape rotates 90 degrees anticlockwise.

The hatching rotates 45 degrees clockwise.

3) Hatching looks the same rotated 90 degrees clockwise or 90 degrees anticlockwise.

Original shapes

90° clockwise rotations

90° anticlockwise rotations

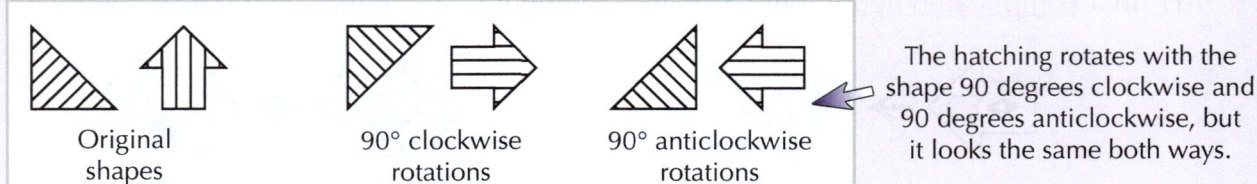

The hatching rotates with the shape 90 degrees clockwise and 90 degrees anticlockwise, but it looks the same both ways.

Practice Questions

1) Which figure is a rotation of the figure on the left? Circle the right letter.

   Rotate

   a   b   c   d

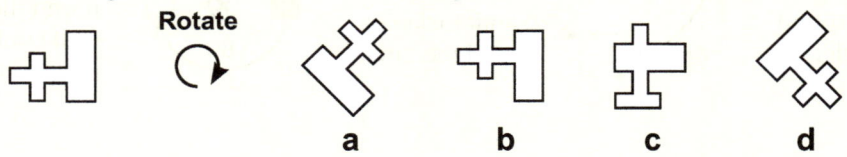

2) Which figure comes next in the series? Circle the right letter.

   a   b   c   d

3) Which figure is the most like the first two figures? Circle the right letter.

   a   b   c   d

Spotting Patterns

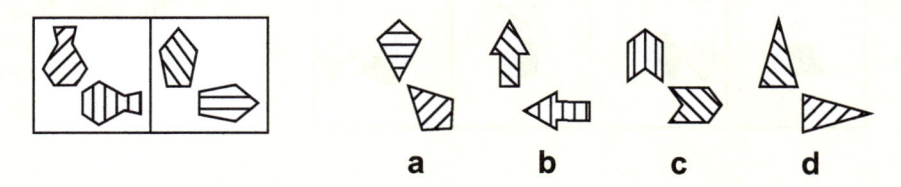

Reflection

If you look in a mirror you will see your reflection. Reflecting a shape or an object is the same idea, except that you're doing it on a piece of paper instead of in a mirror.

Warm-Up Activity

Draw a picture on a piece of paper. Then, try to draw how the picture would look if you held it up to a mirror. Use a real mirror to check how close your drawing was to the reflection.

Reflection is when a shape gets Flipped across a Mirror Line

A reflected shape should look like the original shape as if it was seen in a mirror.

Reflections use a Mirror Line

1) If you were to put a real mirror along a mirror line you would see in the mirror how the original shape should be reflected.

2) The shapes on either side of the mirror line should be identical to each other, except that one has been flipped over.

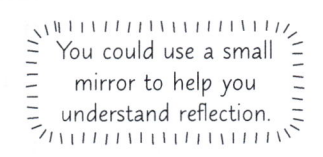

You could use a small mirror to help you understand reflection.

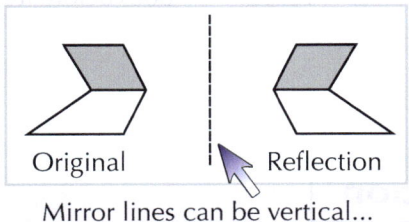

Original / Reflection
Mirror lines can be vertical...
(Shape is reflected across)

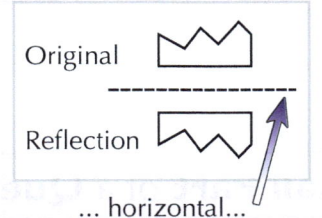

Original / Reflection
... horizontal...
(Shape is reflected downwards)

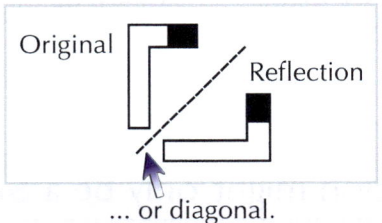

Original / Reflection
... or diagonal.
(Shape is reflected diagonally)

Most Reflection Questions Won't show you a Mirror Line

Spotting that a shape is reflected is half the battle, so it helps to get used to recognising reflections. Think about how shapes would look if they were reflected.

If you work out where the mirror line should go, it will help you see whether one shape is a reflection of another.

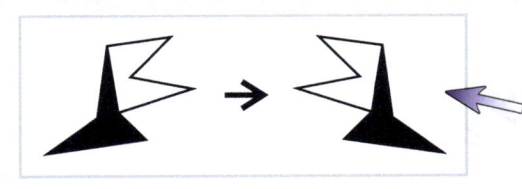

It's obvious that the right-hand figure is a reflection of the left-hand shape.

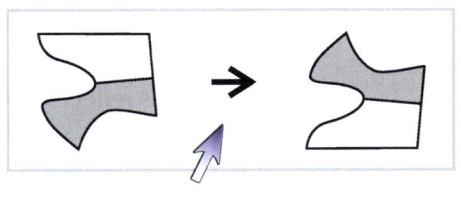

Even though these figures are next to each other, the right-hand shape is a downwards reflection of the left-hand shape.

Even though these figures are next to each other, the right-hand shape is a diagonal reflection of the left-hand shape.

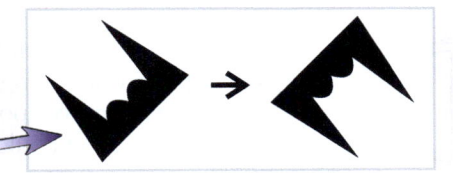

A reflection won't always tell you where the shape should be, only what it should look like.

Spotting Patterns

With Some Shapes it's Hard to Spot a Reflection

Even simple reflections can be a bit tricky — especially if a hatched shape is involved.

1) Some reflected shapes look the same as the original shape.

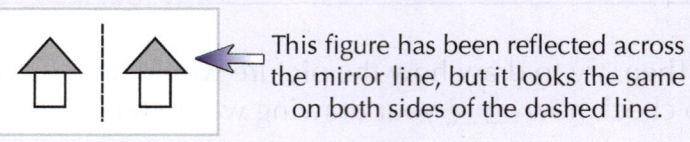

   This figure has been reflected across the mirror line, but it looks the same on both sides of the dashed line.

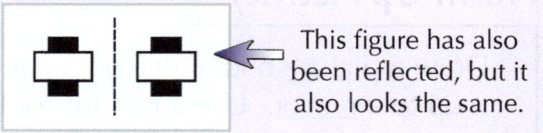

   This figure has also been reflected, but it also looks the same.

2) Hatched shapes might give you a clue as to whether a shape has been reflected, because hatching can also be reflected.

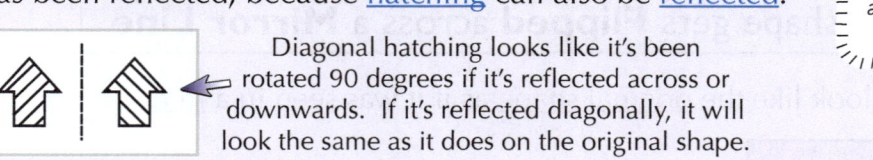

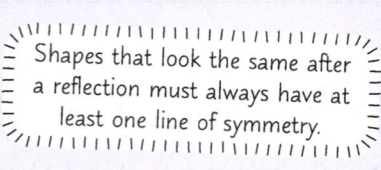

   Diagonal hatching looks like it's been rotated 90 degrees if it's reflected across or downwards. If it's reflected diagonally, it will look the same as it does on the original shape.

   Shapes that look the same after a reflection must always have at least one line of symmetry.

3) Parallelograms only look slightly different if they are reflected — you should be careful not to confuse a reflected parallelogram with a rotated one.

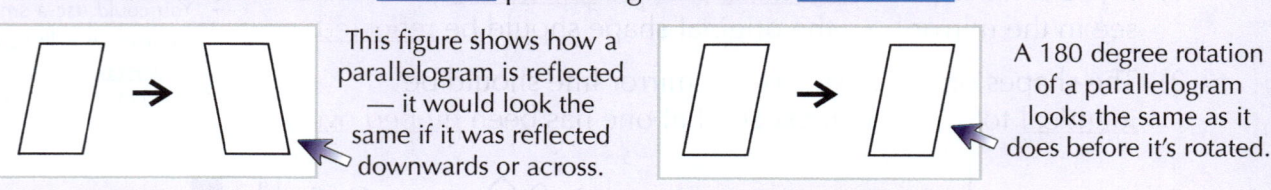

   This figure shows how a parallelogram is reflected — it would look the same if it was reflected downwards or across.

   A 180 degree rotation of a parallelogram looks the same as it does before it's rotated.

Reflection might only be a Small Part of a Question

In complicated questions reflection might only be part of everything that's going on, so you need to check carefully for reflected shapes.

1) In questions where there is a lot happening, it could be easy to miss a reflection.

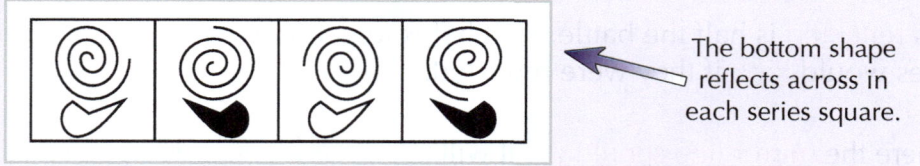

   The bottom shape reflects across in each series square.

2) In some questions you might have to work out how one figure turns into another.

   The black shape in the left-hand figure is reflected downwards in the right-hand figure.

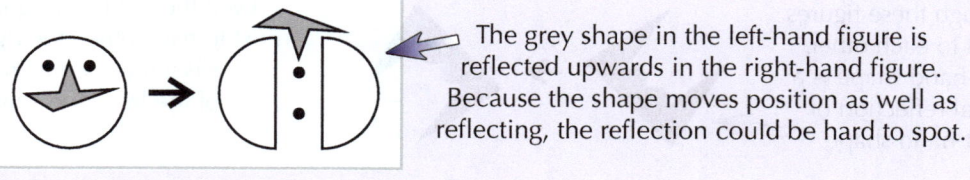

   The grey shape in the left-hand figure is reflected upwards in the right-hand figure. Because the shape moves position as well as reflecting, the reflection could be hard to spot.

Be Careful not to Confuse Reflection with Rotation

See p.7 for more on symmetry.

Rotation and reflection often appear together, so you need to be able to tell the two apart.

Check that a Rotation isn't Hiding a Reflection

Unsymmetrical figures which are reflected cannot be rotated to match the original figure.

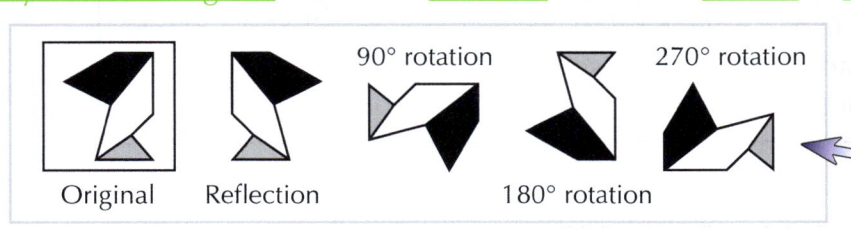

Original   Reflection   90° rotation   180° rotation   270° rotation

No matter how the reflected shape is rotated, it won't look the same as the original.

The circled figure is a reflection of all the other shapes, but this is hidden by its rotation.

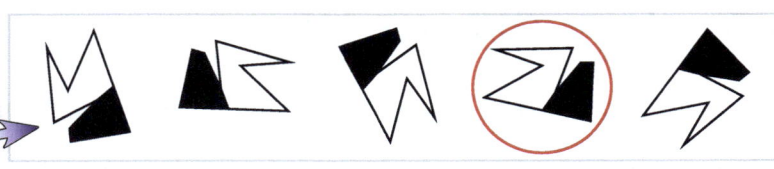

Questions with Reflected shapes that Also Rotate can be Tricky

If a figure rotates and reflects at the same time, it's hard to work out what's happening.

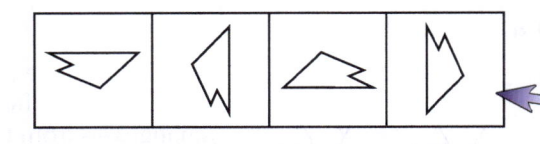

In this sequence the shape rotates 90 degrees anticlockwise each time, then reflects across its longest side. You can tell that it must reflect because no matter how you rotate each shape it won't match the next shape in the sequence.

Practice Questions

1) Which figure is the odd one out? Circle the right letter.

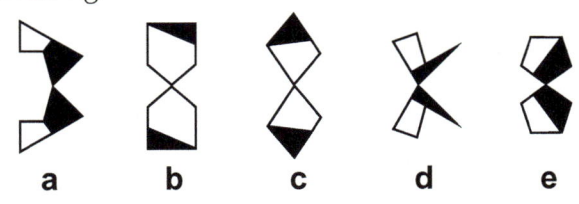

   a   b   c   d   e

2) Which figure is a reflection of the figure on the left? Circle the right letter.

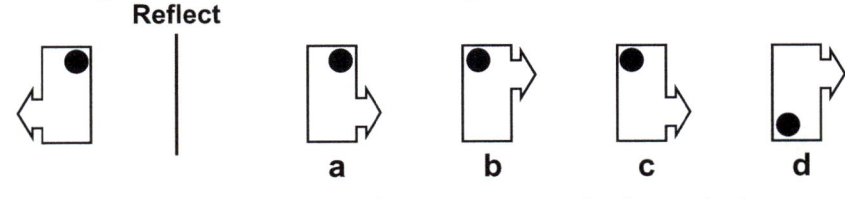

   Reflect

   a   b   c   d

3) Which figure comes next in the series? Circle the right letter.

   a   b   c   d

Spotting Patterns

Layering

Layering is when a shape is in front of or behind another shape. Imagine putting a book on top of another book. If you looked at the pile of books from the side you would see that it has two layers.

Warm-Up Activity

Find five different objects (e.g. a mug, a ruler), as well as a pencil and a piece of paper. Draw around each of the objects so that their outlines overlap. Colour in the parts of your picture where the shapes overlap.

Shapes can Overlap in Different Ways

You might see all the outlines of overlapping shapes, or one shape might be in front of the other.

1) Even without changing position, two shapes can overlap differently.

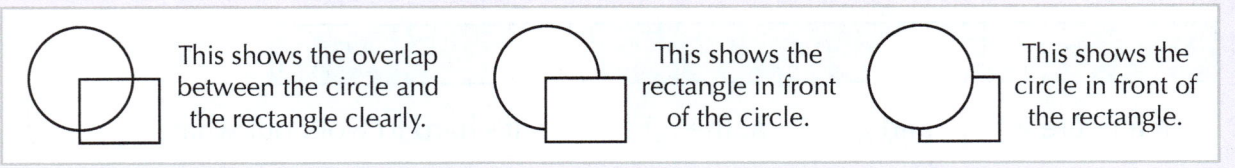

   This shows the overlap between the circle and the rectangle clearly.

   This shows the rectangle in front of the circle.

   This shows the circle in front of the rectangle.

2) The type of overlap shown could be important in a question.

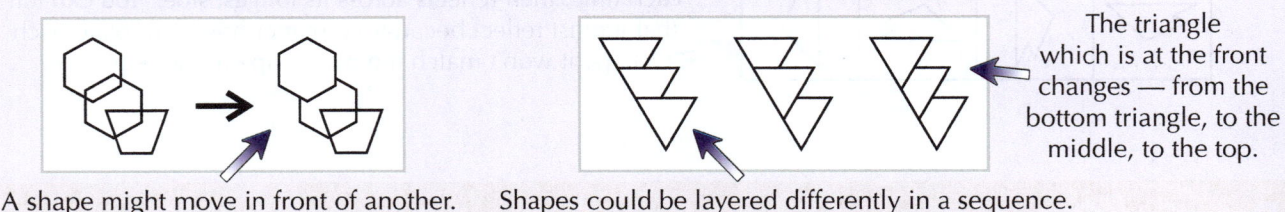

   A shape might move in front of another.

   Shapes could be layered differently in a sequence.

   The triangle which is at the front changes — from the bottom triangle, to the middle, to the top.

The Shapes Created by an Overlap are Important

Try treating the overlap between the two shapes as a separate shape. The shape created by an overlap can look a bit strange, which might help you spot a cut-out shape.

1) When two or more shapes overlap, extra shapes are made.

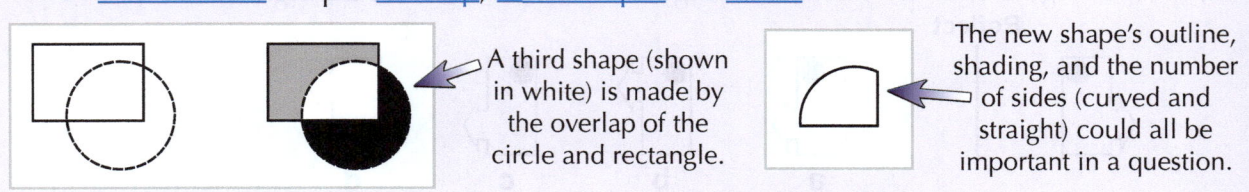

   A third shape (shown in white) is made by the overlap of the circle and rectangle.

   The new shape's outline, shading, and the number of sides (curved and straight) could all be important in a question.

2) In some questions the overlap will be cut out and changed.

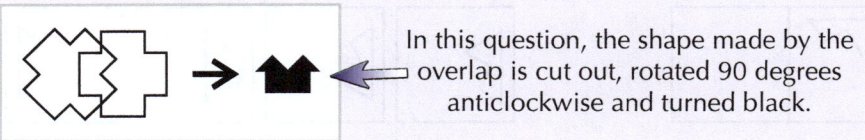

   In this question, the shape made by the overlap is cut out, rotated 90 degrees anticlockwise and turned black.

Spotting Patterns

Shapes can be Ordered by Layer

In questions where shapes overlap it might be important how they are arranged — you should check which shape is at the front and which is at the back.

1) If there are lots of figures that are layered, you could look at what all the shapes at the front or back have in common.

The black shape is at the front of each figure, and the white shape is always at the back.

2) Where two shapes overlap in each figure, the shapes at the front might all be different, but be related to the shapes behind them in the same way.

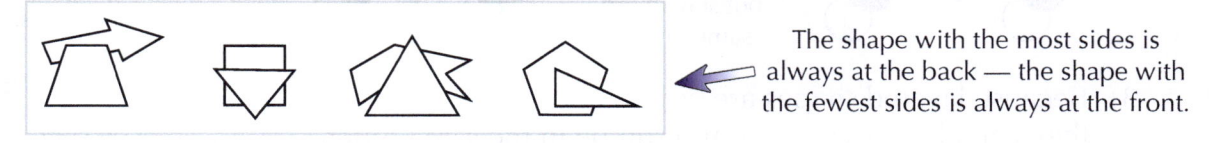

The shape with the most sides is always at the back — the shape with the fewest sides is always at the front.

Some questions will have More Than One Overlap

In questions with lots of overlapping shapes you need to look at more than just the front and back shapes — you also need to look at all the shapes in between.

Look at how Shapes are Layered on top of Each Other

Overlapping shapes can be positioned in different ways.

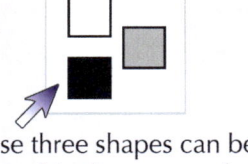

These three shapes can be layered in the same order but in different positions.

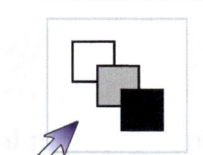

Going diagonally up to the left. From front to back — black, grey, white.

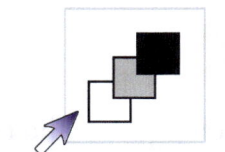

Going diagonally down to the left. From front to back — black, grey, white.

Look at how Every Shape is Layered in a figure

1) Figures can also be layered so that every shape overlaps each other.

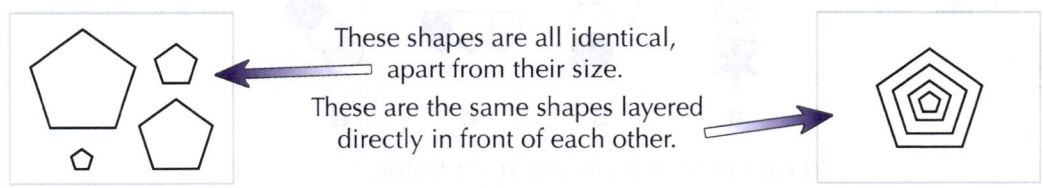

These shapes are all identical, apart from their size. These are the same shapes layered directly in front of each other.

2) Watch out for figures where every shape is layered, but not every shape overlaps.

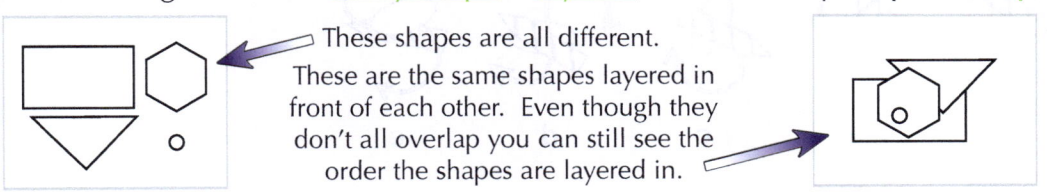

These shapes are all different. These are the same shapes layered in front of each other. Even though they don't all overlap you can still see the order the shapes are layered in.

Spotting Patterns

Layered shapes might Change Position, Layer or Colour

If layered shapes change colour or position, you should double check whether the order of the shapes stays the same or not.

1) Sometimes layered shapes will change without moving.

   These shapes stay in the same position, but the shading moves back (or out) one shape each time.

2) Sometimes layered shapes will move positions or layers.

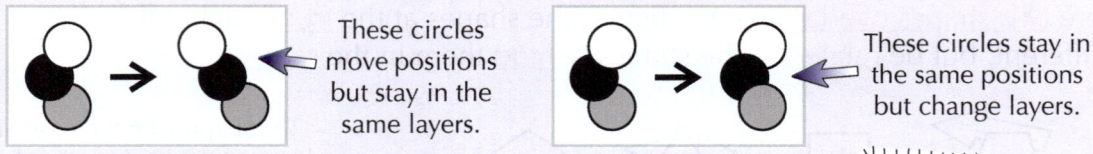

   These circles move positions but stay in the same layers.

   These circles stay in the same positions but change layers.

   See p.18-19 for more about order.

3) Because layered shapes are ordered from front to back they can also move layers and still be in the same order.

   Although all of these figures move positions and layers, they still have the same order — C shape, rectangle, arrow-style line, triangle — they just have different shapes at the front.

Practice Questions

1) Which figure is the odd one out? Circle the right letter.

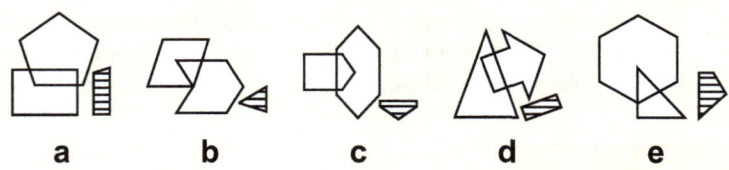

   a   b   c   d   e

2) Which figure is the most like the first two figures? Circle the right letter.

   a   b   c   d

3) Which figure is the odd one out? Circle the right letter.

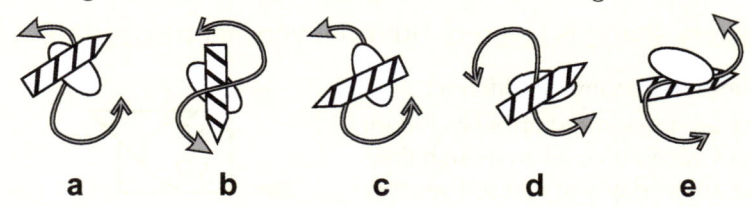

   a   b   c   d   e

Spotting Patterns

Question Types — Similarities and Differences

Similarities and Differences

The questions on this page are all about finding a figure that's the same as or different from another group of figures. They're a bit like spot the difference puzzles... only different.

You'll need to Compare different figures

1) These questions are all about spotting similarities and differences between figures.
2) To find the right answer, you'll have to compare the different elements of the figures, like shading or shape. Look back at pages 4-28 to remind yourself what to look for.
3) There are two types of question in this section:

Odd One Out

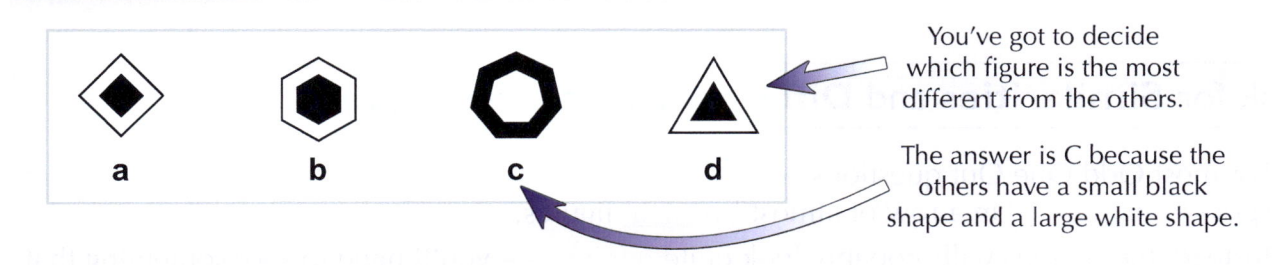

You've got to decide which figure is the most different from the others.

The answer is C because the others have a small black shape and a large white shape.

Find the Figure Like the Others

1) Here's a Find the Figure Like the Others question:

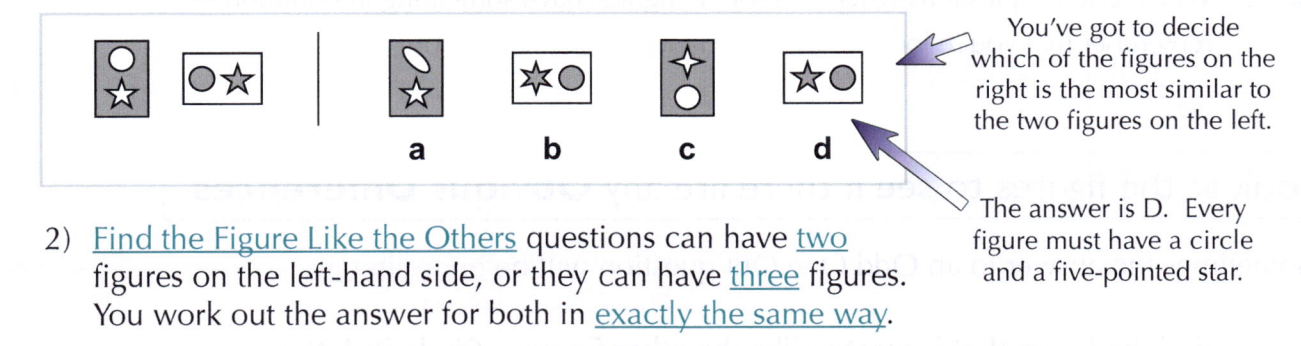

You've got to decide which of the figures on the right is the most similar to the two figures on the left.

The answer is D. Every figure must have a circle and a five-pointed star.

2) Find the Figure Like the Others questions can have two figures on the left-hand side, or they can have three figures. You work out the answer for both in exactly the same way.

Writing Notes can help you learn how to do these questions

Here are some useful tips for starting out with these questions.

1) As you go through the different parts of each question to decide which ones will help you find the answer, write down the ones you've already looked at. This will stop you from looking at the same one twice. If you're stuck on a question, look back at the list of elements on page 4 and see if you're missing any from your list.
2) If you're counting something in each figure (e.g. the number of dots or the number of sides), write down how many you count for each one to help you keep track of the numbers.

These tips are useful when you're learning how to do the questions, but as you get closer to the test, you'll need to learn to keep track of these things in your head.

Odd One Out

For these questions, all you've got to do is spot the odd one out. Sounds pretty easy, but sometimes the pesky thing's hidden really well... Here are some tips to help you hunt it down.

Warm-Up Activity

1. Find another person to play this game with you. Each draw <u>five boxes</u> on a piece of paper and draw a <u>picture</u> inside <u>each box</u>. The pictures should all <u>look different</u>, but <u>four</u> should have something in <u>common</u> that the other one <u>doesn't</u> (e.g. four different cars and one lorry).
2. <u>Cut out</u> the boxes, <u>shuffle</u> them and <u>swap</u> them with the other person.
3. <u>Time</u> how long it takes each of you to find the picture that's <u>different</u> from the other four and say <u>why</u> it's the <u>odd one out</u>. The person who does this the <u>fastest wins</u>.

Look for **Similarities** and **Differences** between shapes

1) For most Odd One Out questions you usually won't have to spot <u>one difference</u> in a row of almost <u>identical</u> figures.
2) Instead, the options will probably look quite <u>different</u> — you'll need to spot something that <u>all but one</u> of the figures have <u>in common</u>. The option that <u>doesn't</u> have it is the <u>answer</u>.

TIPS & TRICKS: Tips and Tricks for Odd One Out questions

Watch out for questions where two of the figures have something in common — remember that you're looking for <u>one</u> shape that's different from <u>all</u> the others.

Look at the figures to see if there are any **Obvious Differences**

Sometimes the answer to an Odd One Out question will be <u>quite simple</u>.

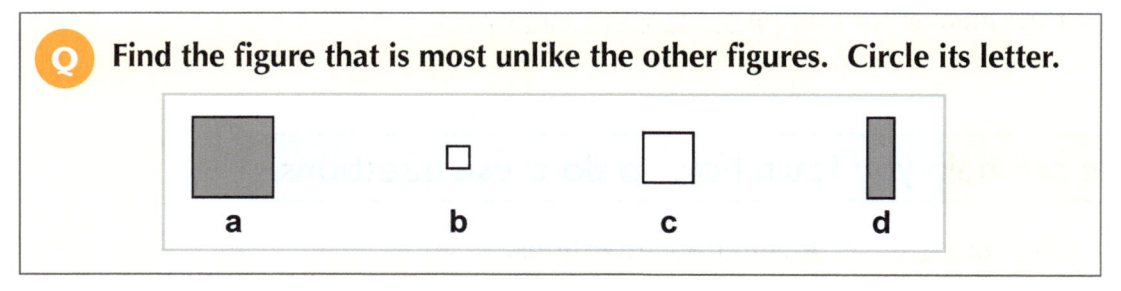

Q Find the figure that is most unlike the other figures. Circle its letter.

a   b   c   d

Method 1 — Look for a simple answer

See if you can spot anything <u>straight away</u> — then quickly <u>check</u> your answer.

1) In this example, the odd one out must be <u>D</u> (a rectangle) because all the other figures are <u>squares</u>.
2) Look at the other elements to make sure you're right. All the shapes are <u>different sizes</u>, so you can't use size to spot the odd one out. Two figures are <u>white</u> and two are <u>grey</u> — this means that shading <u>isn't relevant</u>.

Question Types — Similarities and Differences

If the answer isn't **Obvious**, go through each **Element** one by one

Sometimes you won't be able to spot the odd one out straight away.

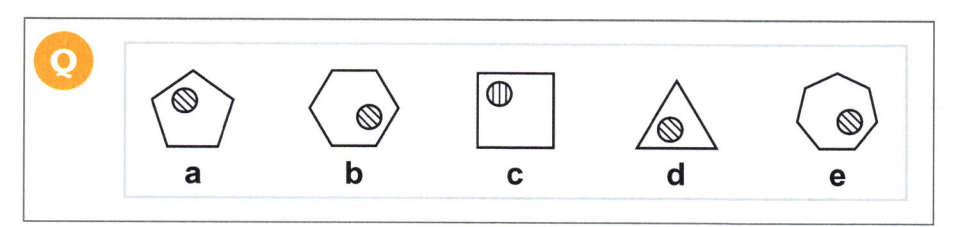

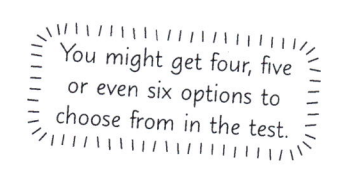

You might get four, five or even six options to choose from in the test.

Method 2 — Look at each element in turn
1) Think about the different elements that can come up (see p.4).
2) Check each one in turn until you find something that four figures share, and one doesn't.

1) Large shapes — they're all different, and there's nothing that four out of five have in common.
2) Small shapes — they're all circles that are the same size.
3) Position — the circles are in different positions in each white shape — position doesn't help you find the odd one out.
4) Shading — the large shapes are all shaded the same. All the small circles are hatched, but only four have the same direction of hatching. C has vertical hatching — the others all have hatching going diagonally down to the right, so the answer is C.

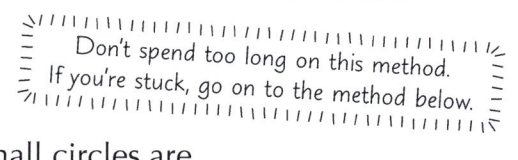

Don't spend too long on this method. If you're stuck, go on to the method below.

Sometimes you'll have to think about **More Than One Element**

In some questions you can only spot the odd one out by looking at a combination of different elements.

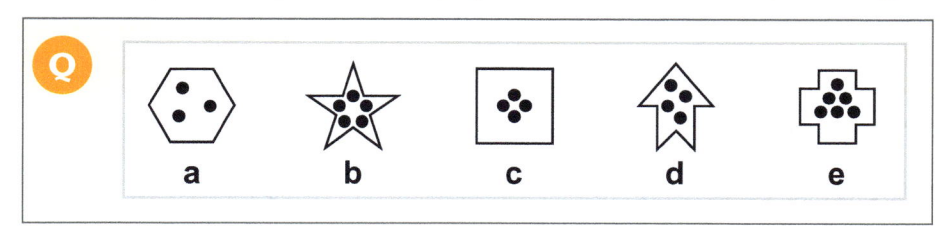

In this example, you could look at the number of sides the shapes have, the number of dots, the size of the shapes and the symmetry of the shapes without finding the answer. You need to try the next method:

Method 3 — Look at more than one element at a time
Look at how the elements work together — try to find links between them.

1) Count the sides of the white shapes — A has 6, B has 10, C has 4, D has 8, and E has 12. They all have different numbers of sides and they are all even, so you need to look at something else.
2) Count the number of black dots — A has 3, B has 5, C has 4, D has 4, and E has 6. You need to find something that four figures have in common, so this doesn't help either.
3) Compare these numbers — A has 6 sides and 3 dots, B has 10 sides and 5 dots, C has 4 sides and 4 dots, D has 8 sides and 4 dots, and E has 12 sides and 6 dots.
4) This shows that the white shapes in A, B, D and E have twice the number of sides as the number of black dots. C has the same number of sides as black dots, so it's the odd one out.

Question Types — Similarities and Differences

Sometimes the answer is **Simpler** than it **Looks**

If you can't find the answer after looking at all the elements in each figure and at different combinations of elements, try looking at the simple things again — some questions are simpler than they look.

Q   Find the figure that is most unlike the other figures. Circle its letter.

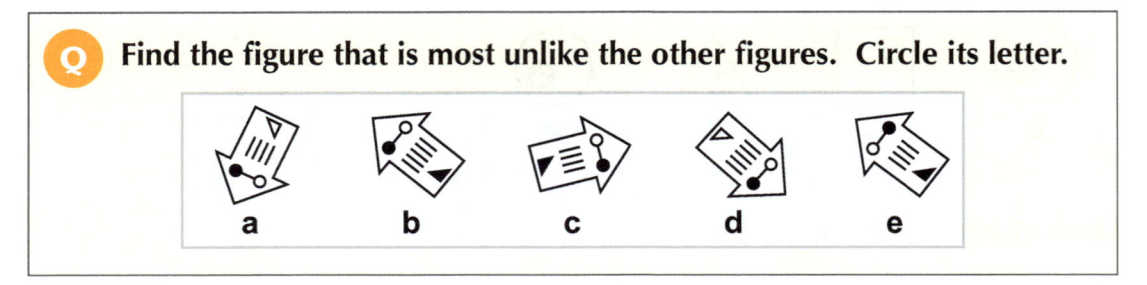

a   b   c   d   e

Go through the elements again, to see if you've missed anything:

1) Number of lines — two figures have five lines and three figures have four lines.
2) Shading of triangle — two figures have white triangles and three have black triangles.
3) Rotation of triangle — all of the triangles rotate with the arrow. None of them are reflected.
4) Shading of circles — every figure has one black circle and one white circle.
5) Position of circles — in A, C, D and E, the black circle is on the right of the shape when the arrow is pointing up. In B it's on the left of the shape. This means that B must be the odd one out.

Tips and Tricks for Odd One Out questions
When the figures all look similar but are rotated differently, it might help to turn the page so you can look at them all the same way up.

Practice Questions

Which figure is the odd one out? Circle the right letter.

1)   a   b   c   d

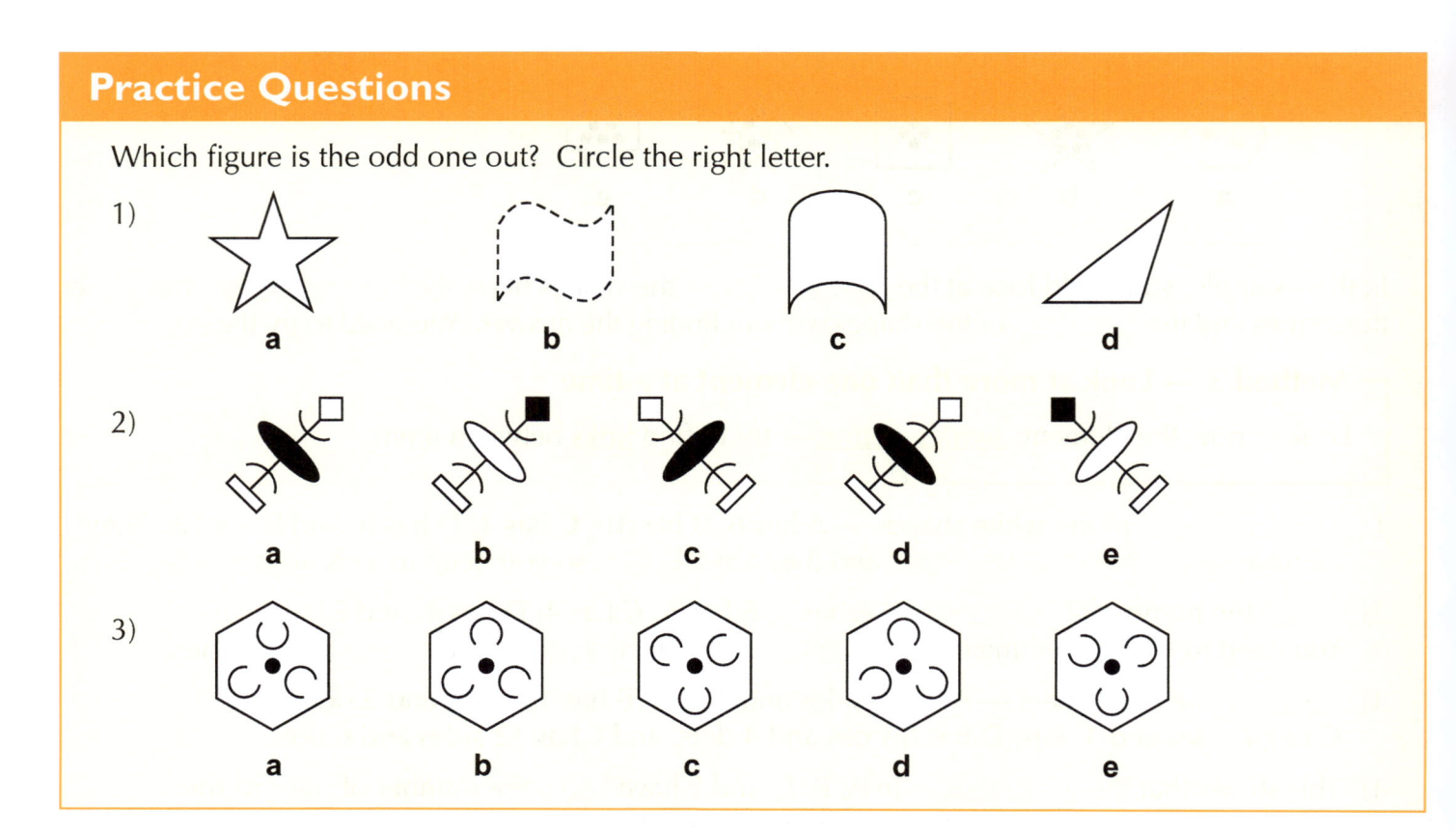

2)   a   b   c   d   e

3)   a   b   c   d   e

Question Types — Similarities and Differences

Find the Figure Like the Others

These questions are a bit like Odd One Out questions — you'll still be spotting similarities and differences — so the skills you practised in the last section will come in handy.

Warm-Up Activity

1. Find another person to play this game with you. Cut a piece of card into 18 squares.
2. Draw each of these shapes on a different square: a large red triangle, a large blue triangle, a large yellow triangle, a small red triangle, a small blue triangle, a small yellow triangle. On the next 12 squares, do the same, but with circles and then rectangles.
3. Shuffle the squares and put them onto a table, face down. Take it in turns to turn over two squares. If they have two things in common (e.g. they're both small and red) you can keep them. If they don't, turn them back over and the other person takes their turn.
4. The winner is the person with the most cards when you can't make any more pairs.

The Answer has something In Common with the Example Figures

1) For these questions, you need to find something that all the example figures on the left of the page have in common, which only one of the answer options has too. That option is the answer.
2) You might get questions with two or three example figures. You can use the same method to answer both types of question.
3) The answers might all look quite different. Remember that you're not trying to find the one that looks most like the examples — look for the only one with the right elements in common with them.

Sometimes you'll Only need to look at One Element

Look at the most obvious things first — they might give you the answer, or narrow down the options.

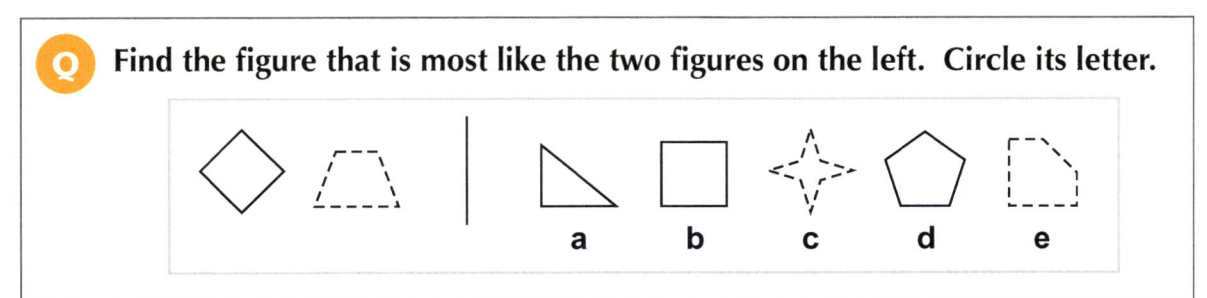

Q Find the figure that is most like the two figures on the left. Circle its letter.

Method 1 — Look for obvious similarities
1) Find one thing that all of the example figures have in common.
2) If only one of the answer options also has that thing in common, then that must be the answer.

1) Both example figures are white, but all the options are also white, so that doesn't help. Each example figure has a different type of line, so that's not something they have in common.
2) Both example figures have four sides. Only one of the options has four sides — the answer is B.

Question Types — Similarities and Differences

You might need to look at **A Few** elements **Separately**

Often the example figures will have a few elements in common, that may not be linked. Instead of looking for all the similarities at once, use the method below.

> **Q** Find the figure that is most like the three figures on the left. Circle its letter.
>
> a   b   c   d

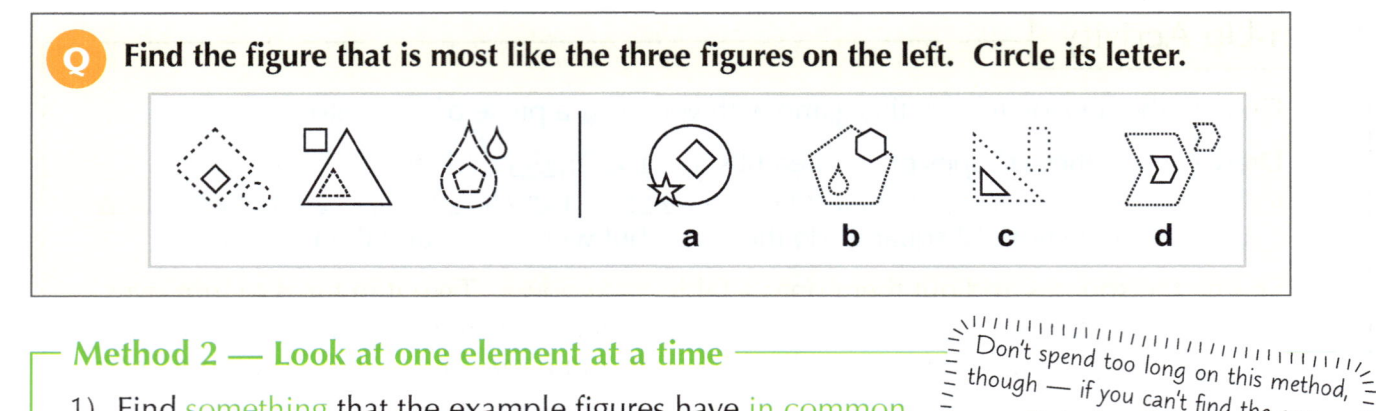

Method 2 — Look at one element at a time

1) Find something that the example figures have in common.
2) Rule out the answer options that don't have the same element.
3) Repeat these two steps until you're only left with one option — that's the answer.

Don't spend too long on this method, though — if you can't find the answer, go on to the next method.

1) Type of line — in each figure, the large shape has the same type of line as one of the small shapes. This rules out A (all of the shapes have the same type of line).
2) Small shapes — in each figure, only one of the small shapes must be the same as the big shape. This rules out D (all the shapes are the same) and B (they're all different). The answer is C.

The similarity could be a **Link** between **Two Elements**

If it's not obvious what the examples have in common, look at how different elements are related.

> **Q**
>
> a   b   c   d   e

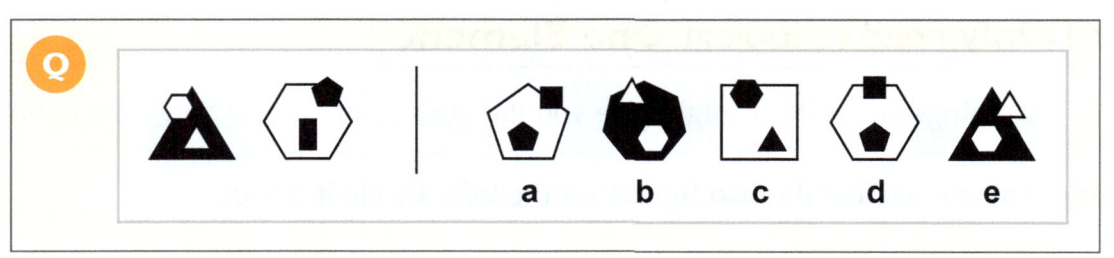

In this example, looking at the elements separately doesn't help you find the answer.

Method 3 — Look for links between the elements

Look at the different elements in the example figures to see if there are any links between them.

1) There aren't any links between the number of sides of the large shape and the two small shapes.
2) You could add up the number of sides of the two small shapes, but that doesn't help — the sides of the small shapes in both of the figures and all of the options add up to nine.
3) In the first example figure, the small shape at the top has six sides and the small shape below it has three. In the second figure, the small shape at the top has five sides and the small shape below it has four. The shape with the most sides is always on top.
4) Only option C has the shape with the most sides at the top — it must be the answer.

Question Types — Similarities and Differences

You **Might** need to **Look** for a **Pair** of **Rules** to find the **Answer**

1) For some questions, you might need to work out a pair of rules. The rules could be something like — 'If the shape is a square then it's white. If it's a circle then it's black'. The answer will be the only option which follows this rule.

2) Only look for rules if you can't solve the question any other way — rule questions are very rare.

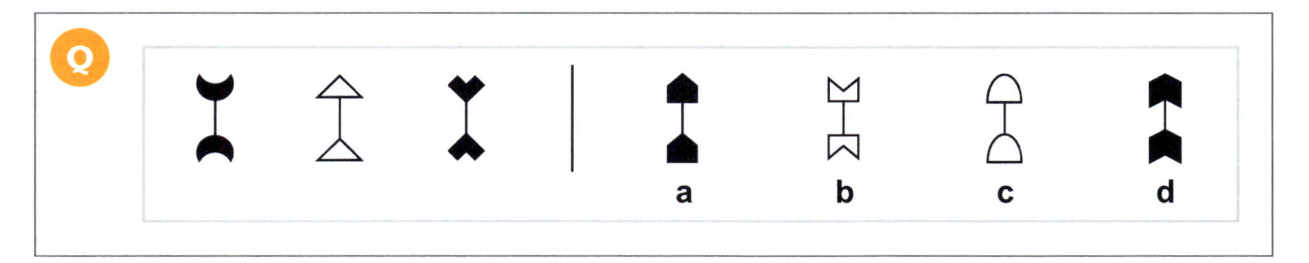

Method 4 — See if the example figures follow a pair of rules

1) Look for one example figure that has two differences from the other two example figures. In the middle example figure, the shapes at the end of the line are white, and have the same rotation, and in the others the shapes are black and are 180 degree rotations of each other.

2) Try to make a pair of rules out of these two differences. The rules in the example could be — 'If the shapes are white, then they have the same rotation. If they're black then they're 180 degree rotations of each other.'

Odd One Out questions can have rules too, e.g. if the circle is inside the shape it's white, and if it's outside it's black. The odd one out breaks the rule (the circle might be white and outside).

3) If only one of the answer options follows this pair of rules, then that's the answer. The only answer option to follow this rule is C, so this must be the answer.

Practice Questions

Which figure is most like the two figures on the left? Circle the right letter.

1)

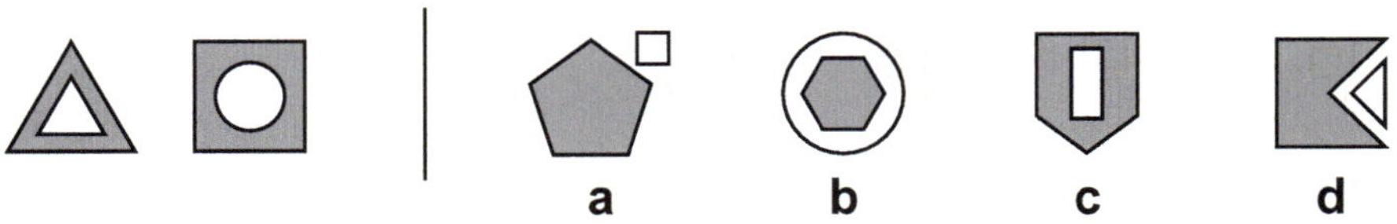

Which figure is most like the three figures on the left? Circle the right letter.

2)

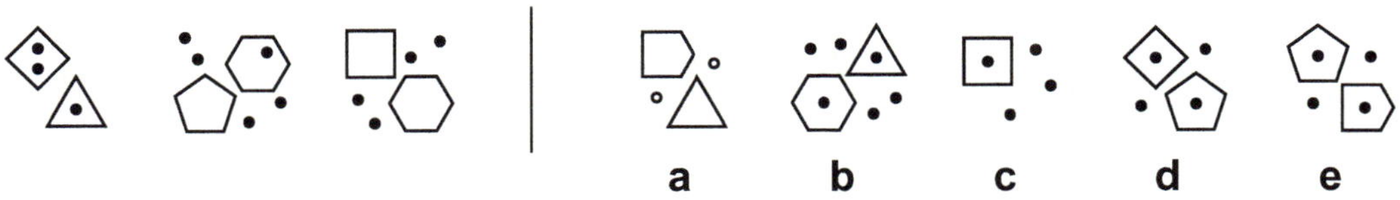

3)

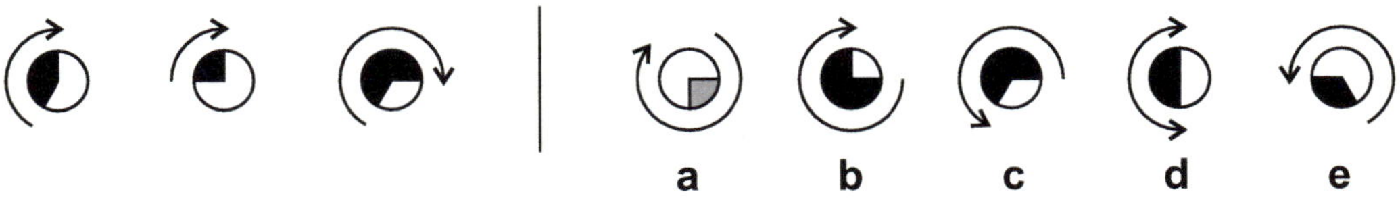

Question Types — Similarities and Differences

Question Types — Pairs, Series and Grids

Pairs, Series and Grids

These pages are about Complete the Pair, Complete the Series and Complete the Grid questions. Don't get your snap cards out yet, though — Complete the Pair isn't quite that fun...

You'll need to spot How Figures Change

1) These questions are all about spotting **changes** between figures.
2) Once you've spotted the change, you'll have to change **another** figure in the **same way**.
3) There are **three** main types of question in this section:

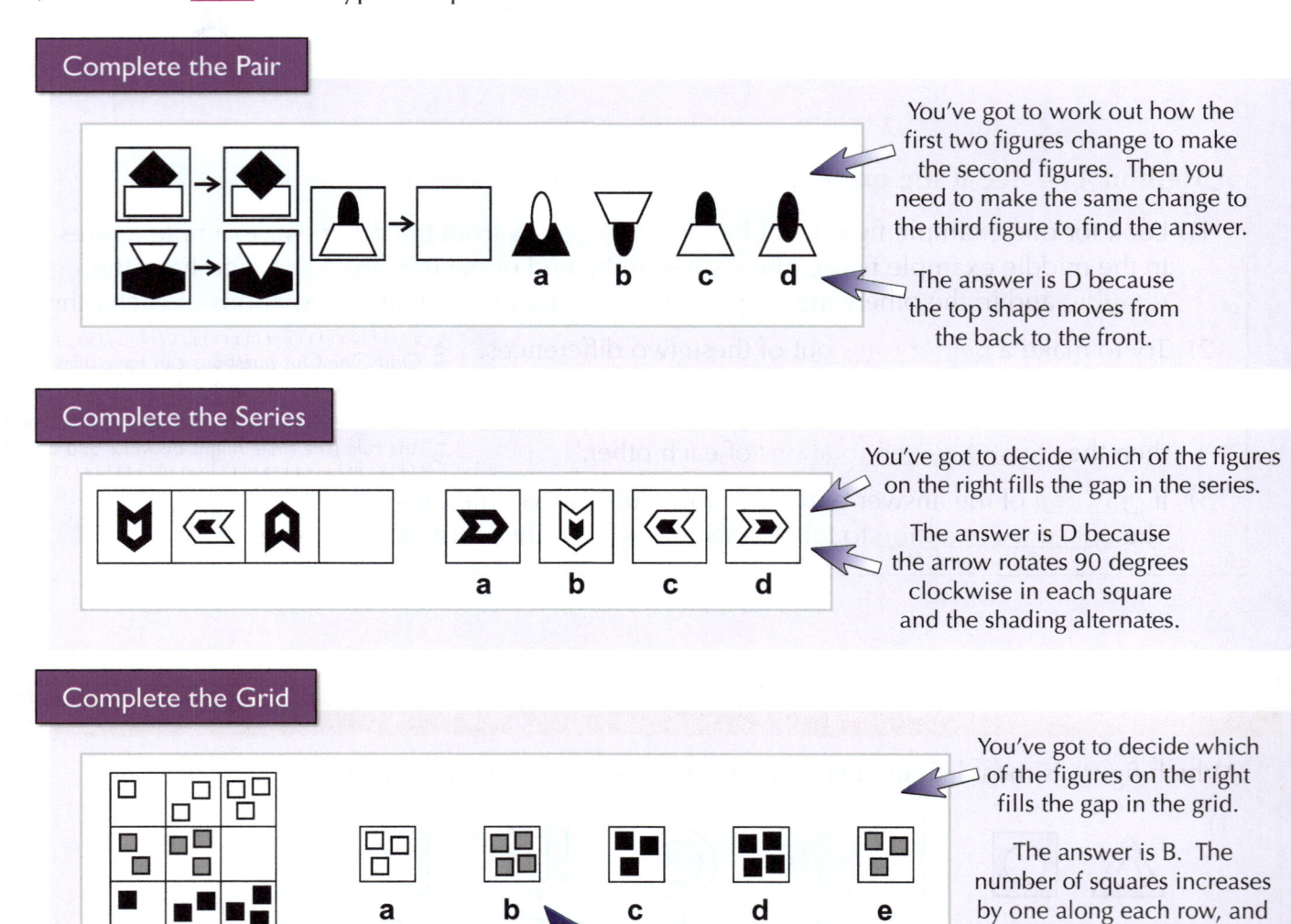

Complete the Pair

You've got to work out how the first two figures change to make the second figures. Then you need to make the same change to the third figure to find the answer.

The answer is D because the top shape moves from the back to the front.

Complete the Series

You've got to decide which of the figures on the right fills the gap in the series.

The answer is D because the arrow rotates 90 degrees clockwise in each square and the shading alternates.

Complete the Grid

You've got to decide which of the figures on the right fills the gap in the grid.

The answer is B. The number of squares increases by one along each row, and all the squares in a row are the same colour.

Drawing the Missing Figure or Writing Notes can help you get started

These questions can be tricky at first, so here are some **tips** to help you **improve**:

1) Try **drawing** what you think should go in the **gap** in the series or grid, or what you think the **missing half** of the pair should look like. This'll help you to **imagine** what the answer should be.
2) You could also **write down** each **change** that you spot between the figures to **keep track** of them.

When you're more **confident** about these questions, and you're getting **close** to the **test**, you'll need to keep track of the changes and work out what the answer looks like **in your head**.

Complete the Pair

In these questions, you've got to be able to spot how figures change to make other figures. There might be a few changes to notice, but don't worry — just look at them one at a time.

Warm-Up Activity

1. Find another person to play this game with. Each of you should draw two boxes on a piece of paper. Inside the first box, draw a picture (or a collection of shapes) and colour it in. In the second box, draw the same picture, but change four things about it.
2. Swap pictures, and take it in turns to spot the four differences between the two pictures and describe them to your partner. Time how long it takes each of you — the winner is whoever does it the fastest.

Work out how the First figures Turn Into the Second figures

1) For Complete the Pair questions you'll be given two pairs of figures. You've got to work out which element, or combination of elements, changes in the first figures to make the second figures. Then you've got to change another figure in exactly the same way to get the answer.
2) The first two pairs of figures might look very different from the third figure and the options. Remember that you're not looking for the option that's most similar to the other two pairs.

You might only need to spot One Change

In easier Complete the Pair questions, only one thing will change between the first and second figures.

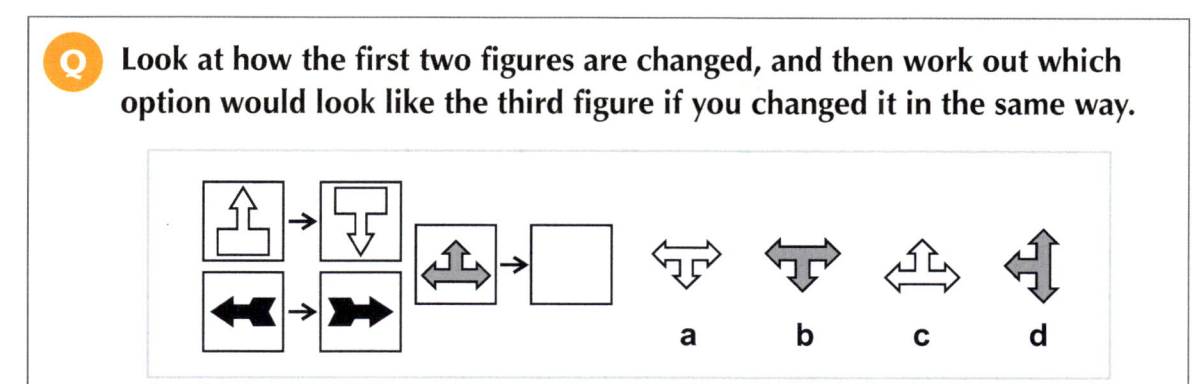

> **Q** Look at how the first two figures are changed, and then work out which option would look like the third figure if you changed it in the same way.

Method 1 — Look at the elements that change
1) First work out what happens to the first figures to make the second figures.
2) Then do the same thing to the third figure to find the answer.

1) In this example, the first figures are rotated 180 degrees to give the second figures.
2) If you rotate the third figure 180 degrees you get the answer — option B.

Question Types — Pairs, Series and Grids

For some questions you'll have to spot **More Than One Change**

In harder Complete the Pair questions, more than one thing will change between each pair.

> **Q** Look at how the first two figures are changed, and then work out which option would look like the third figure if you changed it in the same way.

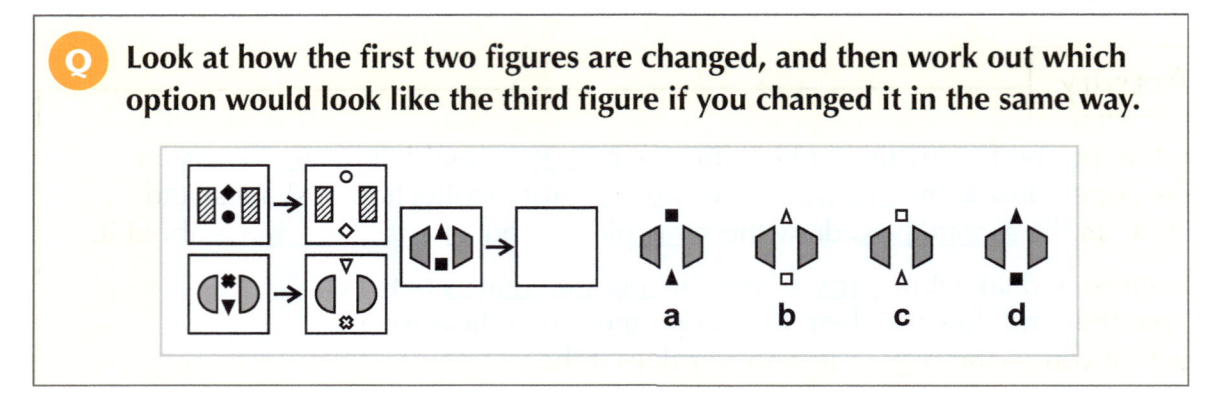

Method 2 — Narrow down the options

If more than one thing changes, use each change to rule out some possible answers.

1) Small shapes — the small shape at the top of the first figure in each pair moves to the bottom in the second figure, and the small shape at the bottom moves to the top. This means that the answer must have a square at the top and a triangle at the bottom. This rules out B and D.
2) Shading — the small shapes change from black to white. This rules out A — the answer is C.

The two **Halves** of each pair might **Look** very **Different**

Sometimes there will be a big change between the first figure and the second figure of the pair.

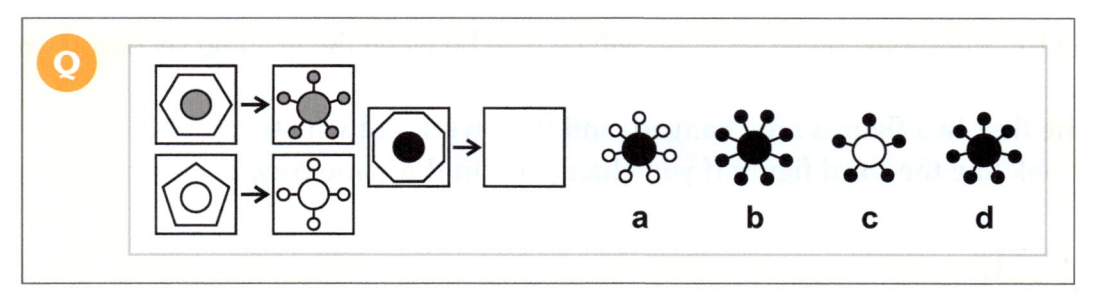

1) Shading — all the circles in the second figures have the same shading as the circle in the first figures. This means that the answer must have only black circles, which rules out A and C.
2) Number of small circles — in both of the second figures there is one less small circle than the number of sides that each white shape has. The white shape in the third figure has eight sides, so the answer must have seven small circles — the answer is D.

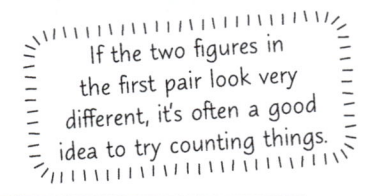

If the two figures in the first pair look very different, it's often a good idea to try counting things.

Tips and Tricks for the Test

If you're allowed to write on the test paper, put a line through the options you've ruled out. If you're not allowed, try putting one finger under every option, and then taking away your fingers as you rule them out. You'll end up pointing at the right answer.

Some questions might look **Very Different**

Sometimes questions might look completely different — you can solve them in the same way though.

> **Q** **Look at how the first bug changes to become the second bug. Then work out which option would look like the third bug if you changed it in the same way.**

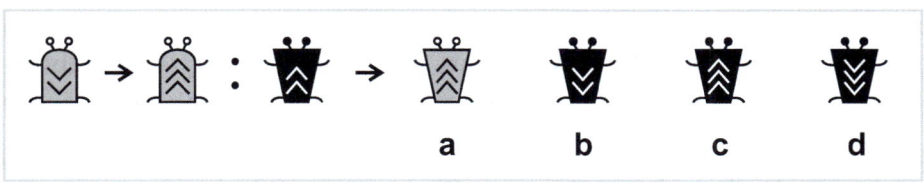

1) Shading — the bug's body and antennae don't change colour, which rules out option A.
2) Number of lines — one extra v-shaped line is added to the bug's body.
   This means that the answer must have three v-shaped lines, which rules out option B.
3) Rotation — the v-shaped lines on the bug's body rotate 180 degrees.
   This rules out option C, so the answer must be D.

TIPS & TRICKS

Tips and Tricks for Complete the Pair questions

It's easy to confuse 'Complete the Pair' questions with a 'Find the Figure Like the Others' question (p.33-35). In this example, A is more similar to the first pair — it's there to confuse you. Remember what type of question you're answering.

Practice Questions

Look at how the first two figures have been changed. Which option on the right would look like the third figure if you changed it in the same way? Circle the right letter.

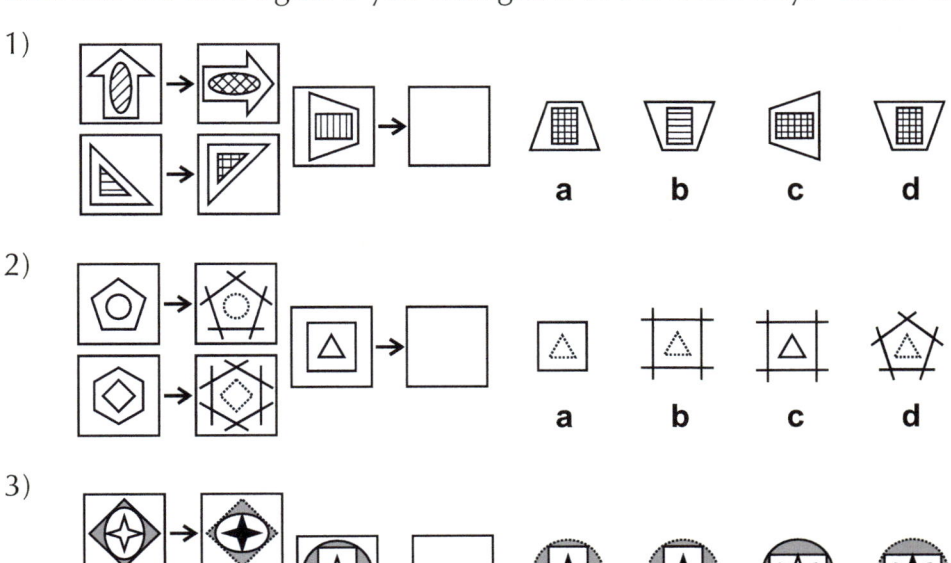

1)

2)

3)

Question Types — Pairs, Series and Grids

Complete the Series

For Complete the Series questions you've got to find the figure that completes a series. You'd never have guessed. These questions are all about sequences and patterns.

Warm-Up Activity

1. Find another person to play this game with you. Each of you should draw a line of four boxes on a piece of paper. Inside the boxes, draw a sequence of pictures of things that happen in order — it could be getting up in the morning, doing the washing-up, etc.

2. Cut up the lines of boxes, shuffle them and then swap them over. Time how long it takes to put the pictures back in the right order. The person with the shortest time wins.

You have to find the Missing Figure in a Series

In Complete the Series questions, you'll be given a set of four or five figures in order, with one figure missing. You've got to choose the option that fills the gap.

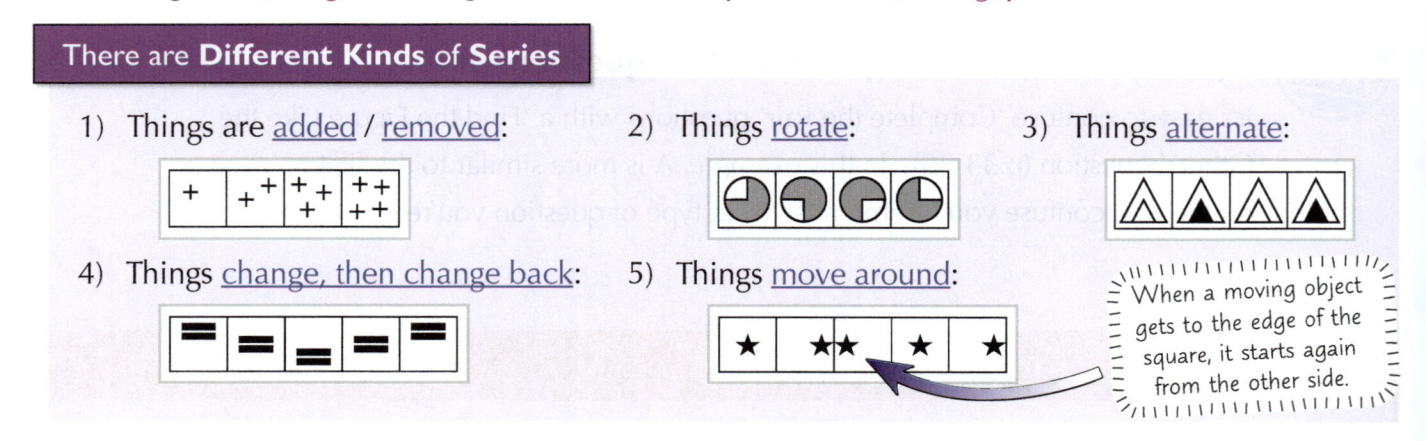

There are Different Kinds of Series

1) Things are added / removed:

2) Things rotate:

3) Things alternate:

4) Things change, then change back:

5) Things move around:

When a moving object gets to the edge of the square, it starts again from the other side.

Work Out what the Pattern is

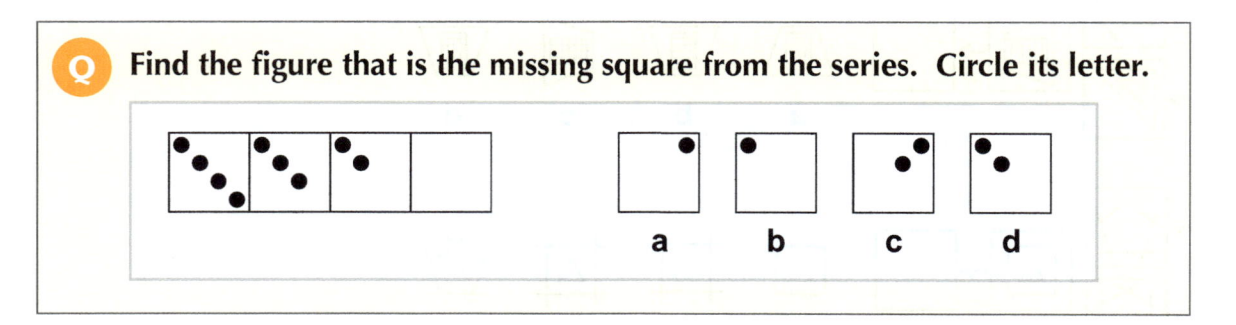

Q Find the figure that is the missing square from the series. Circle its letter.

a   b   c   d

Method 1 — Find the rule

Look at any elements that change in the sequence, and work out the rule.

The only element that changes in this series is the number of circles — the bottom right-hand circle is taken away in each series square. The circles that are left stay in the same corner of the series square. This means that the answer must be B because it has one circle in the top left-hand corner.

You might have to find **More Than One Pattern**

Some questions have more than one element that changes. Each change could follow a different rule. Look at each element separately to see if it changes, and how it changes.

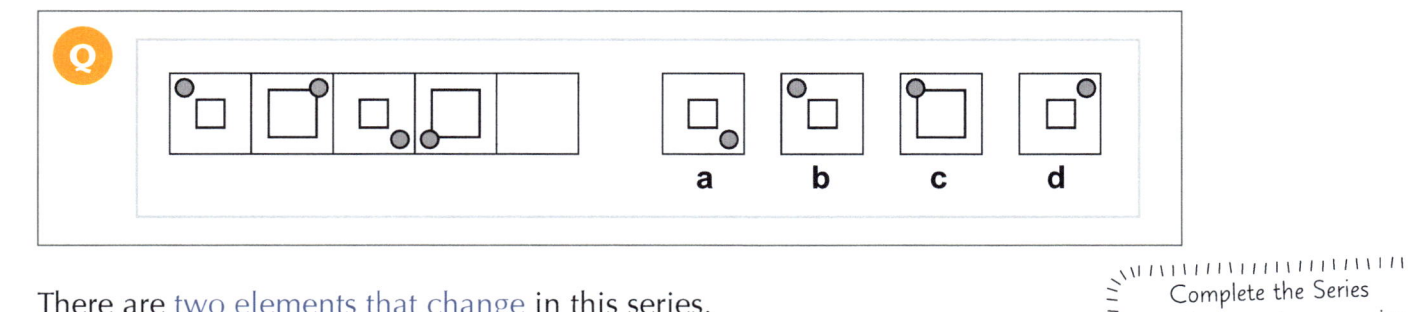

Q

There are two elements that change in this series.
1) Size of shape — the size of the squares alternates between small and big. The fifth figure must have a small square, which rules out C.
2) Position — the circle moves around the corners of the series squares in a clockwise direction. This means that the fifth figure will have a circle in the top left-hand corner, so the answer is B.

Complete the Series questions can have a series with four or five squares.

It **Won't Always** be the **Last Square** that's missing

1) Any of the figures in the series could be missing. If the first figure is missing, you might have to work backwards from the end of the series to the beginning to find the answer.
2) If one of the middle figures is missing, look at the figures on either side of the missing square for clues.

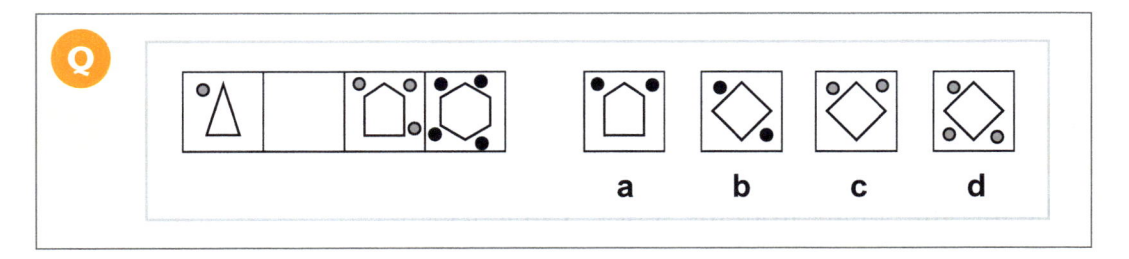

Q

Method 2 — Look at the figures before and after the missing square

Look at each element that changes in the series:

1) Shape — counting the number of sides of the white shapes gives the sequence: 3, ?, 5, 6. The sequence must be an adding sequence which goes: 3, 4, 5, 6 — the missing shape must have 4 sides. This rules out A.

2) Number of circles — counting the number of circles gives the sequence: 1, ?, 3, 4 — it goes up by one in each square. The missing square must have two circles — this rules out D.

3) Colour of circles — looking at the three figures in the sequence tells you that the colour of the circles alternates between black and grey. The first figure has a grey circle, so the answer must have black circles. This rules out C, so the answer must be B.

Question Types — Pairs, Series and Grids

Some sequences can look very **Strange**

Sometimes looking at the whole sequence doesn't help — try splitting it into two halves.

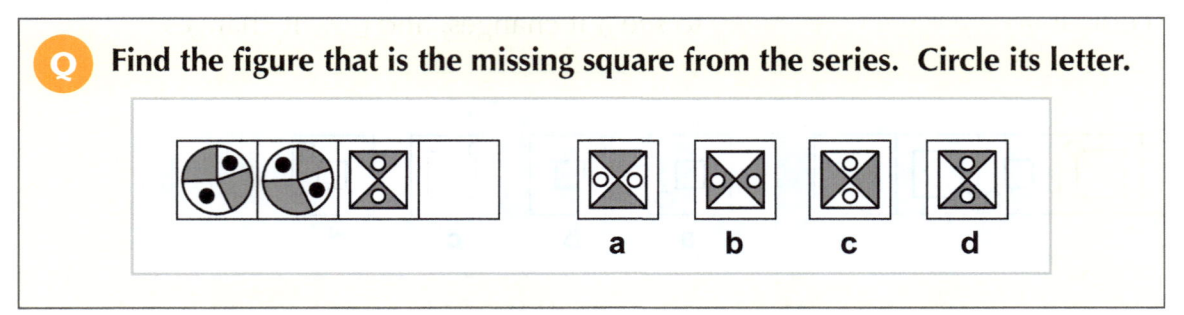

> **Q** Find the figure that is the missing square from the series. Circle its letter.
>
> [sequence of four squares with the fourth missing, followed by options a, b, c, d]

In this example you can see what changes between the first and second squares, but the figure in the third square looks very different. You need to try the next method.

Method 3 — Only look at the first two squares
1) Look at what changes between the first square and the second square.
2) Work out what the third square would look like if it was changed in the same way.

1) Shading — the four sections of the circle in the first figure swap shadings in the second figure. This means the missing figure must have the opposite shading to the third figure (the sections on the right and the left must be grey). This rules out A and D.

2) Position of dots — the dots in the first two figures are always in the white parts of the circle. In the third figure, the dots are in the grey parts of the shape. This means that the dots in the missing figure must also be in the grey parts of the shape. This rules out C, so the answer must be B.

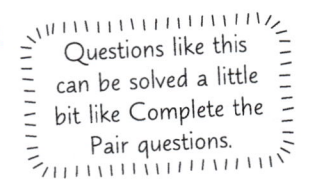

Questions like this can be solved a little bit like Complete the Pair questions.

Practice Questions

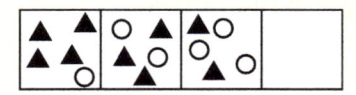

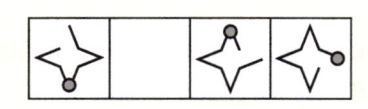

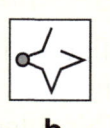

Find the figure that is the missing square from the series. Circle its letter.

1) [sequence of pentagon shapes with options a, b, c, d]

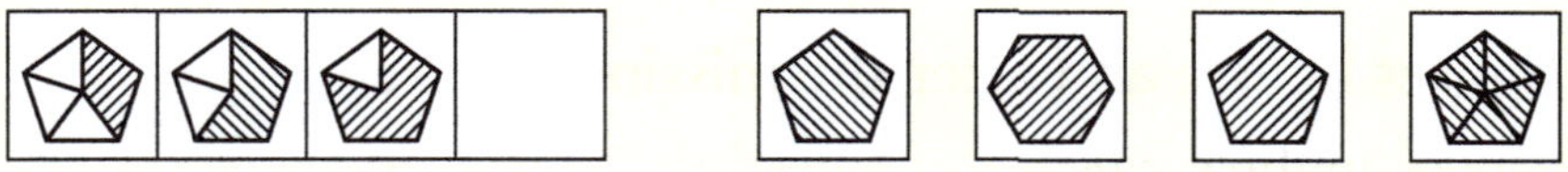

2) [sequence with triangles and circles with options a, b, c, d]

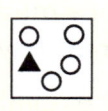

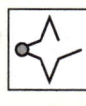

3) [sequence with star shapes and dots with options a, b, c, d]

Question Types — Pairs, Series and Grids

43

Complete the Grid

So the bad news is you've still got one more question type to get your head around in this section. The good news is that it's time for Complete the Grid, and everyone loves a grid.

Warm-Up Activity

1. Find another person to play this game with you. Each draw a grid three squares high and three squares wide on a piece of paper. Draw a picture that fills all the squares of the grid.
2. Cut up the grid, pick one of the squares and keep it separate from the others.
3. Try to rearrange the other person's squares to make the original picture (with a gap where the missing square should go). When you've made the picture, draw what you think should go in the missing square on another piece of paper.
4. The winner is the person whose drawing is closest to what's on the missing square.

You have to find the Missing Figure in a Grid

1) For Complete the Grid questions, you'll get a grid made up of either squares or hexagons.
2) One of the squares or hexagons in the grid will be blank.
3) You've got to find the figure that fills the blank space in the grid.

Start by looking Along the Rows of a Square Grid

Rows go from side to side. Columns go up and down.

The first thing you should do is look along a complete row to see what happens to each element.

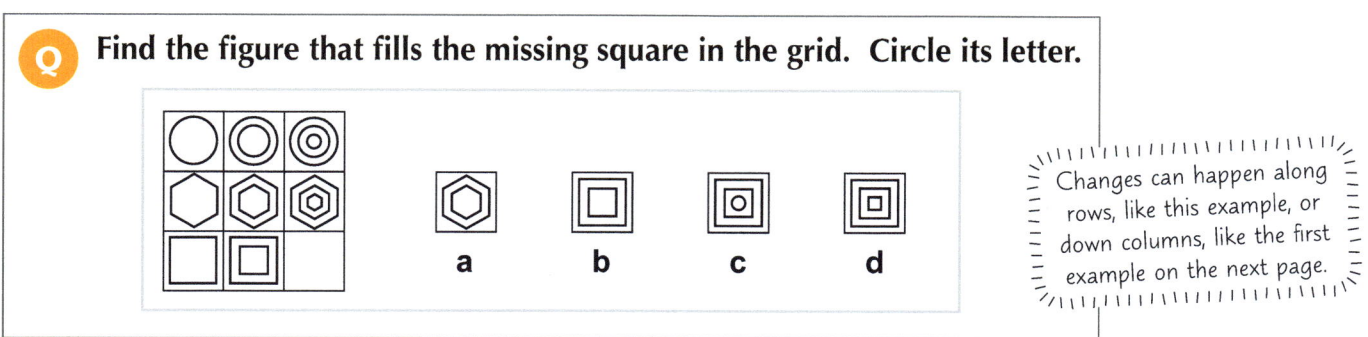

Q Find the figure that fills the missing square in the grid. Circle its letter.

Changes can happen along rows, like this example, or down columns, like the first example on the next page.

Method 1 — Find out what changes along each row

1) Look at a row with no gaps and work out what elements change.
2) To find the missing grid square, make the same changes to the row with the gap.

1) In this example, moving from left to right along the top row, a smaller version of the circle is added in each grid square.
2) To find the missing square, make the same changes to the bottom row of the grid. The bottom row has squares in it, so that rules out A and C. The third column must have one more square than the second column, so that rules out B. The answer must be D.

Question Types — Pairs, Series and Grids

You might have to look for changes Down a Column

This example works down the columns, instead of across the rows. You can work out what goes in the missing grid square in exactly the same way — just spot what's changed in the columns without gaps.

Q Find the figure that fills the missing square in the grid. Circle its letter.

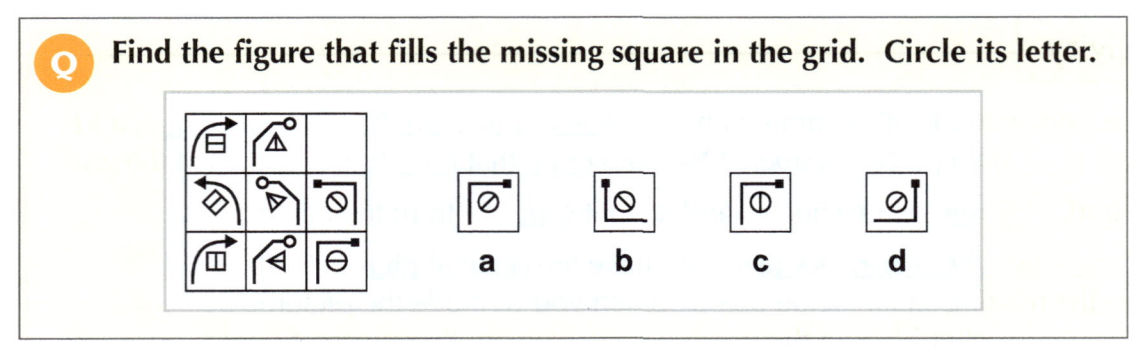

    a   b   c   d

1) In this example, it's difficult to see any connection between the figures along each row — the figures are very different. To find the answer, you need to look down the columns.

2) Looking down the left-hand column, the arrow-style line reflects across. The square rotates 45 degrees anticlockwise going down the column.

3) The missing square is at the top of the grid, so you'll need to move up the right-hand column to find the answer — you'll have to make the changes backwards.

4) The arrow-style line in the middle right-hand grid square must reflect across to make the top right-hand grid square. The circle must rotate 45 degrees clockwise (because you're moving up the column instead of down it). The answer is C.

Grids can work Horizontally and Vertically at the Same Time

In some questions looking at just the columns or the rows won't give you the answer.

Q

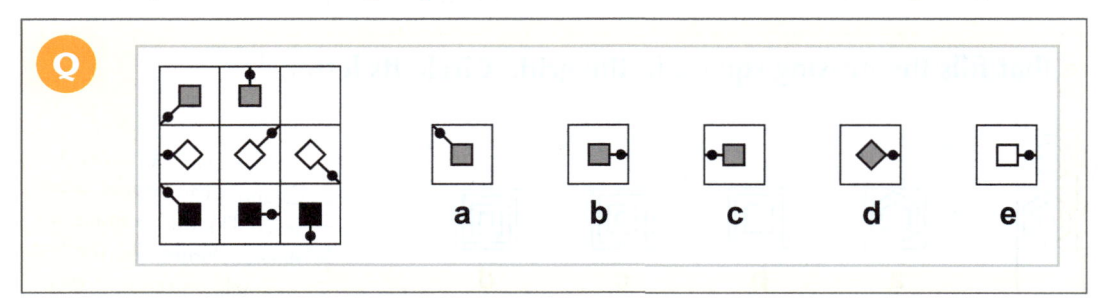

    a   b   c   d   e

Method 2 — Look at the rows and the columns

Look at the rows first, and rule out as many options as you can. Then look at the columns.

1) In each row, all three small squares are shaded and rotated the same. This rules out D and E, but you're still left with three possible answers.

2) Going down each column, the black dot and the line rotate 45 degrees clockwise around the grid square.

3) The missing square is at the top of a column, so you've got to work backwards to find the answer — moving anticlockwise from the grid square below, the black dot must be in the middle on the right. The answer is B.

Treat each row and column as a 3-part series — spot patterns just like you would in a Complete the Series question.

Question Types — Pairs, Series and Grids

The Figures in a Square Grid might make a Pattern

There are a few different types of pattern you need to look out for.

Different Kinds of Pattern

1) Two figures alternate. 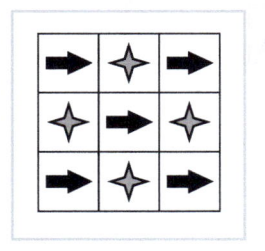
2) Each row moves along.

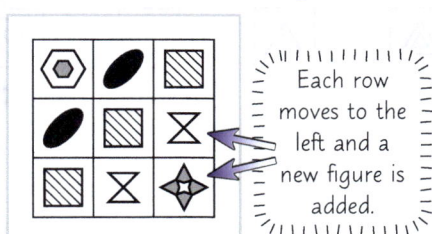

    Each row moves to the left and a new figure is added.

3) The grid makes a big picture.

4) Each element only appears once in each row, once in each column, or once in each row and column.

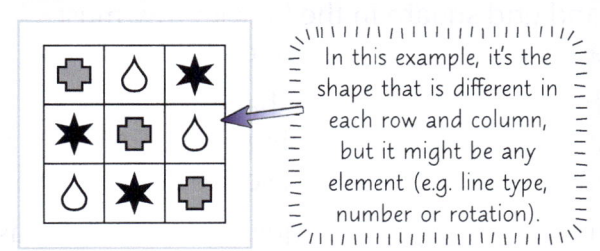

    In this example, it's the shape that is different in each row and column, but it might be any element (e.g. line type, number or rotation).

5) Two different elements each appear only once in each row and column.

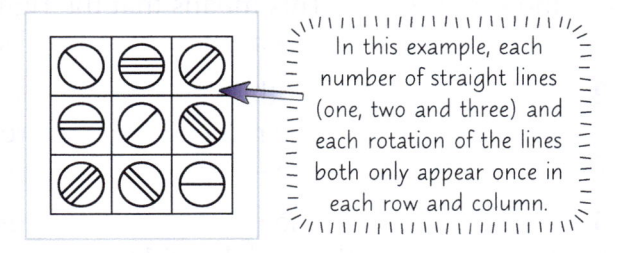

    In this example, each number of straight lines (one, two and three) and each rotation of the lines both only appear once in each row and column.

Grids often have More Than One Pattern or Sequence to look for

The patterns above might be combined with other patterns or sequences.

Q

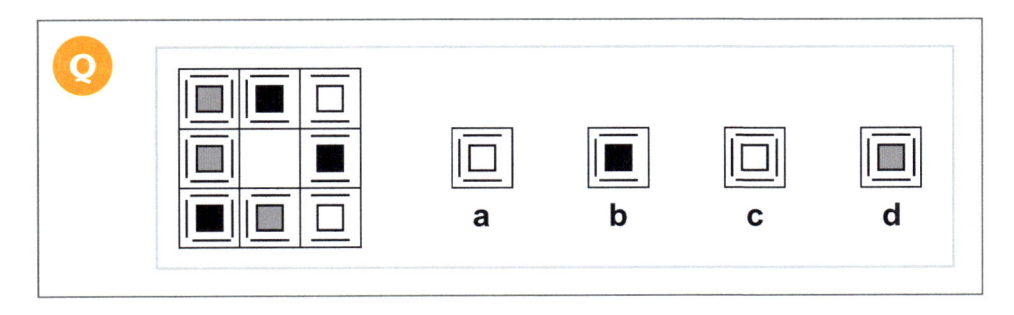

a   b   c   d

When the middle grid square of a row or column is missing, you'll have to look at the grid squares around it to find the answer.

1) In this example, along the top and bottom rows (from left to right) the number of lines changes from four, to three and then to two. The missing grid square is in the middle of a row, so it must have three lines. This rules out C and D.
2) Each shading of square (black, grey and white) only appears once in each row. This means the answer must be white. This rules out B, so the answer must be A.

Question Types — Pairs, Series and Grids

Two grid squares might be Added Together to make the third

In some questions, the contents of two of the grid squares are added together to make the third one.

Q Find the figure that fills the missing square in the grid. Circle its letter.

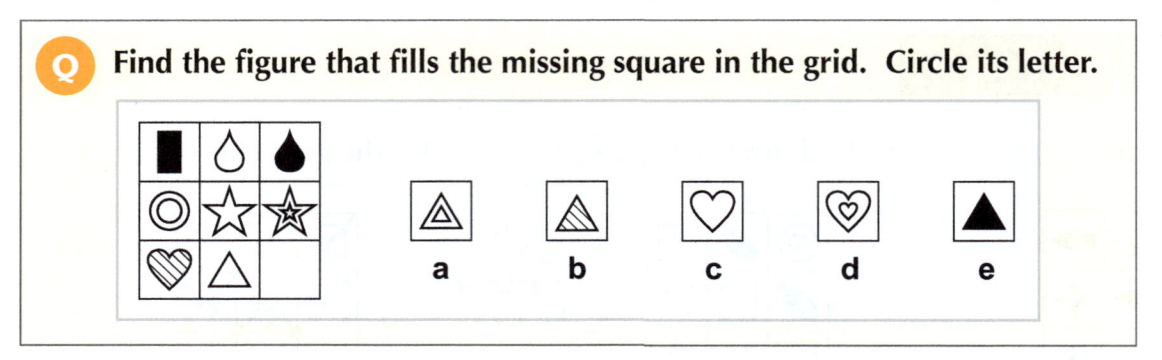

Method 3 — Look for figures that share elements with other figures

If you can't see a sequence or pattern in the grid, check the complete rows and columns for one figure that has elements from the other two figures in the same row or column.

1) In the top two rows of this example, the middle and right-hand grid squares both have the same shape. This means that the right-hand grid square in the bottom row must have the same shape as the middle grid square — a triangle. This rules out C and D.

2) In the top two rows, the left-hand and right-hand grid squares both have the same shading, so the missing grid square must have the same shading as the bottom left-hand grid square — it must be hatched. This rules out A and E, so the answer is B.

3) For this example, the rule is that the figure in the right-hand grid square in each row has the same shape as the middle grid square, and the same shading as the left-hand grid square.

Sometimes the grid might be made up of Hexagons

Q Find the figure that fills the missing hexagon in the grid. Circle its letter.

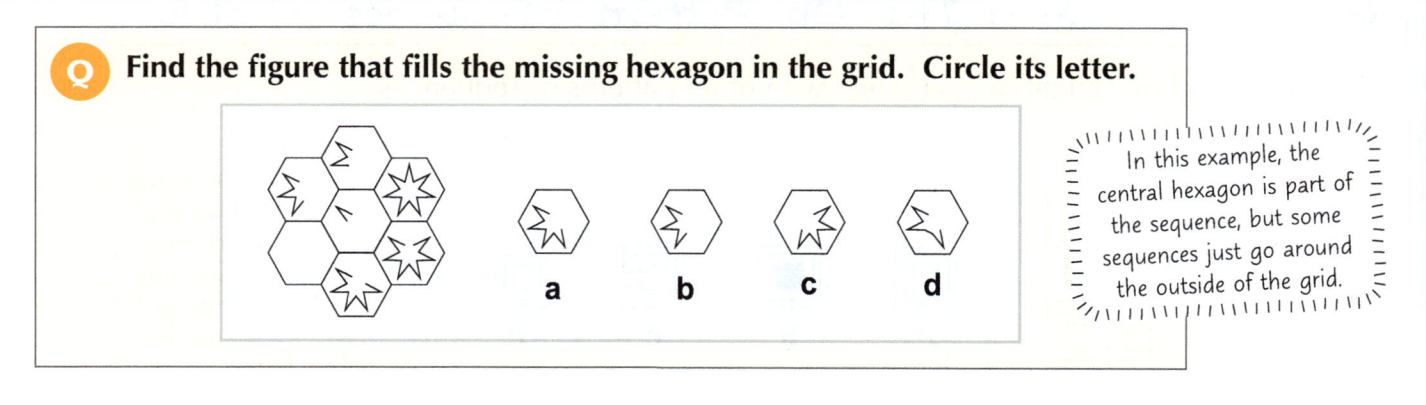

In this example, the central hexagon is part of the sequence, but some sequences just go around the outside of the grid.

Method 4 — Look at what changes from hexagon to hexagon

Look around the outside of the grid and try to work out what changes in each hexagon.

1) Starting from the top hexagon and going anticlockwise, each shape inside the hexagon has one more point than the one that comes before it.

2) There are three points before the missing hexagon and five points after it. The missing hexagon must have four points — this rules out B and D.

3) The points are added in an anticlockwise direction. This rules out C — the answer is A.

Question Types — Pairs, Series and Grids

The Figures in a Hexagonal Grid might make a Pattern

Here are a few of the patterns you'll need to recognise in hexagonal grid questions.

Different Kinds of Pattern

1) Identical shapes on opposite sides.

   Make sure you don't confuse these two kinds of pattern — they can look quite similar.

2) Shapes reflect across the centre.

3) The whole grid makes a big picture.

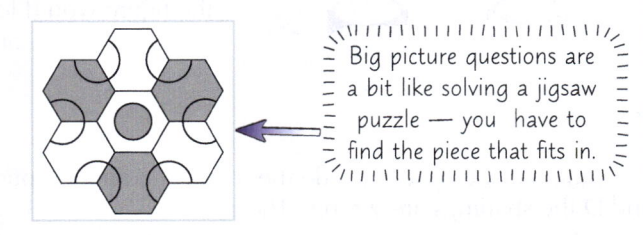

   Big picture questions are a bit like solving a jigsaw puzzle — you have to find the piece that fits in.

4) Two figures alternate.

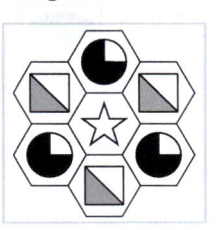

Practice Questions

Which figure fills the missing space in the grid? Circle the right letter.

1)

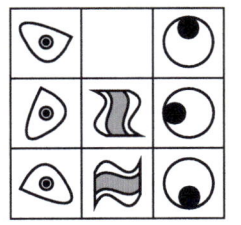

2)

3)

Question Types — Pairs, Series and Grids

Rotation and Reflection

This section is about recognising when shapes have been rotated or reflected. These two transformations can sometimes be tricky to tell apart, so read on for some handy tips.

You'll need to Imagine what Objects look like Rotated or Reflected

1) You'll be shown a figure and asked which of the options is that figure after a rotation or reflection.
2) There are two types of question in this section.

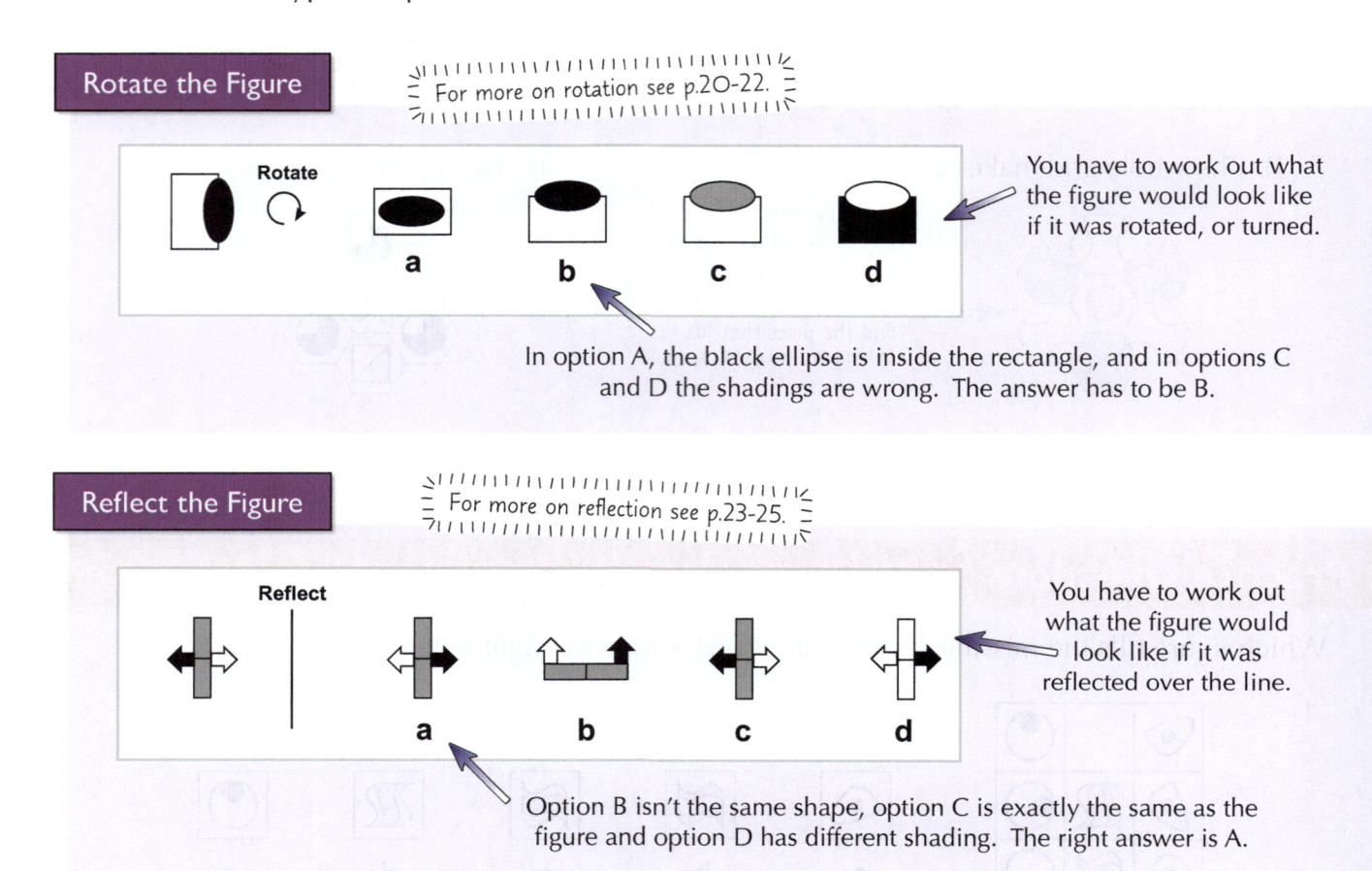

Rotate the Figure

For more on rotation see p.20-22.

You have to work out what the figure would look like if it was rotated, or turned.

In option A, the black ellipse is inside the rectangle, and in options C and D the shadings are wrong. The answer has to be B.

Reflect the Figure

For more on reflection see p.23-25.

You have to work out what the figure would look like if it was reflected over the line.

Option B isn't the same shape, option C is exactly the same as the figure and option D has different shading. The right answer is A.

Investigating how objects Rotate and Reflect can be a big help

These questions can look a bit tricky at first, so here are some tips to get you started:

1) Try drawing round one of the figures above, using tracing paper if you have some. Then turn the paper around, to see what the figure looks like when it's been rotated.
2) If you're using tracing paper, you can also flip the paper over to see what the figure looks like when it's been reflected.
3) If you have a small mirror, you can put it beside a shape to see what its reflection looks like.

The key to rotation and reflection questions is practice. Practise using these tips at first until you can spot a rotated or reflected shape just by looking at it.

Rotate the Figure

In rotation questions, you'll be shown a shape and you have to work out which one of the options is a rotation of the same shape. Sounds easy enough, but it can get tricky.

Warm-Up Activity

1. Find another person to play this game with you. Each of you should draw five shapes down the side of a sheet of paper. (Try not to make them too simple or too complicated.) Swap sheets and try to draw the other person's shapes upside down.
2. Cut out the shapes and turn them around to compare them to the first drawings. The person who draws the most rotations correctly is the winner.

The Answer is the Same as the Example Figure

1) The right answer will be the option which is exactly the same as the example figure but rotated, or turned. All the other options won't be exactly the same.
2) If you imagine rotating the example figure, it will eventually look exactly the same as one of the options — that option is the answer.

Look at the Options to see if there is an Obvious Answer

Some questions might have quite simple shapes — see if you can spot an obvious answer.

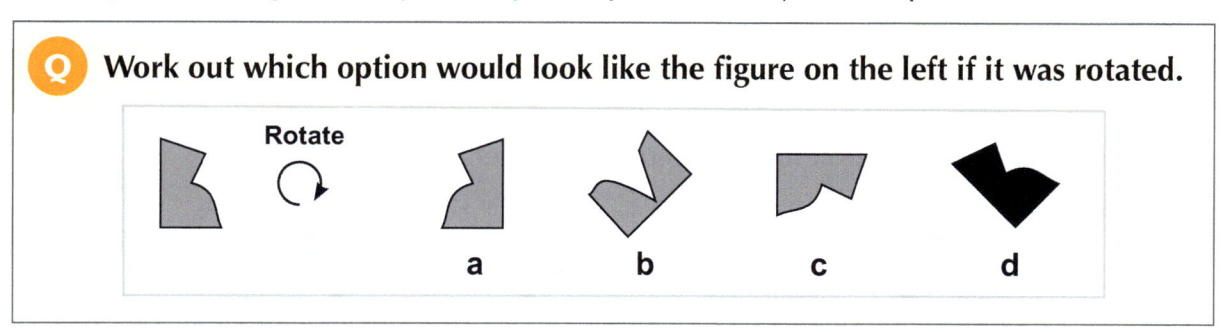

Q Work out which option would look like the figure on the left if it was rotated.

Rotate

a   b   c   d

Method 1 — Look for a simple answer

Look at the example figure and see if you can spot an option straight away which might be the rotated shape — then quickly check your answer.

1) C looks like the figure rotated 90 degrees clockwise, so check that this is right.
2) A is a reflection of the figure on the left, so you can rule it out.
3) You can rule out B because it's not the same shape.
4) You can rule out D because it's a different colour.

Question Types — Rotation and Reflection

Sometimes you might need to Narrow Down the Options

The figure you need to rotate might be quite complicated — it might be two or more shapes together.

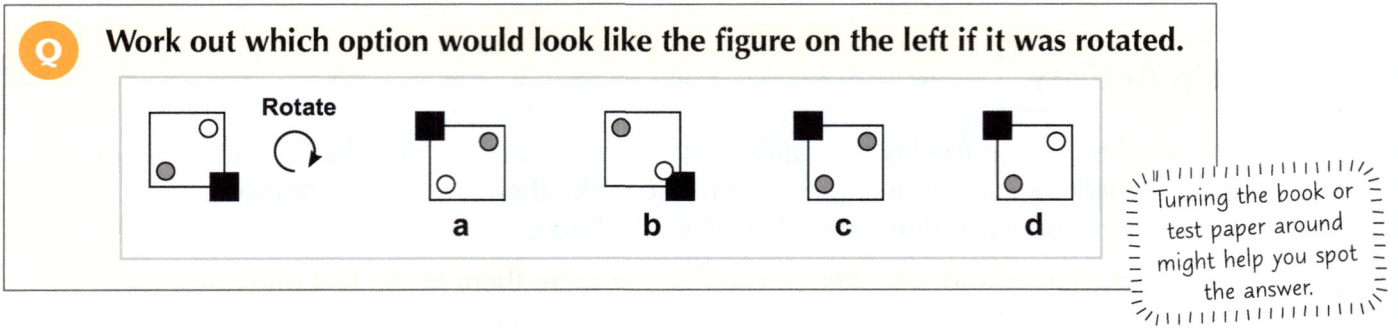

Q Work out which option would look like the figure on the left if it was rotated.

a   b   c   d

Turning the book or test paper around might help you spot the answer.

Method 2 — Rule out the wrong answers one by one
1) Look at each option in turn and try rotating it to see if it matches up with the example figure.
2) Rule out options which don't match up until you're left with one option that does.

1) In B, the black square is in the wrong place, so you can rule it out. The figure on the left has one grey dot and one white dot, but C has two grey dots, so you can rule it out.

2) You can rule out D because it's a reflection and then rotation of the example figure. (If you rotate the figure so that the black square is in the right place, the colours of the dots will be wrong.) That leaves A as the correct answer — it's been rotated 180 degrees.

TIPS & TRICKS **Tips and Tricks for Rotate the Figure questions**
First look for options which have the wrong shape or shading. Then, check any other options to see whether they have been reflected as well as rotated.

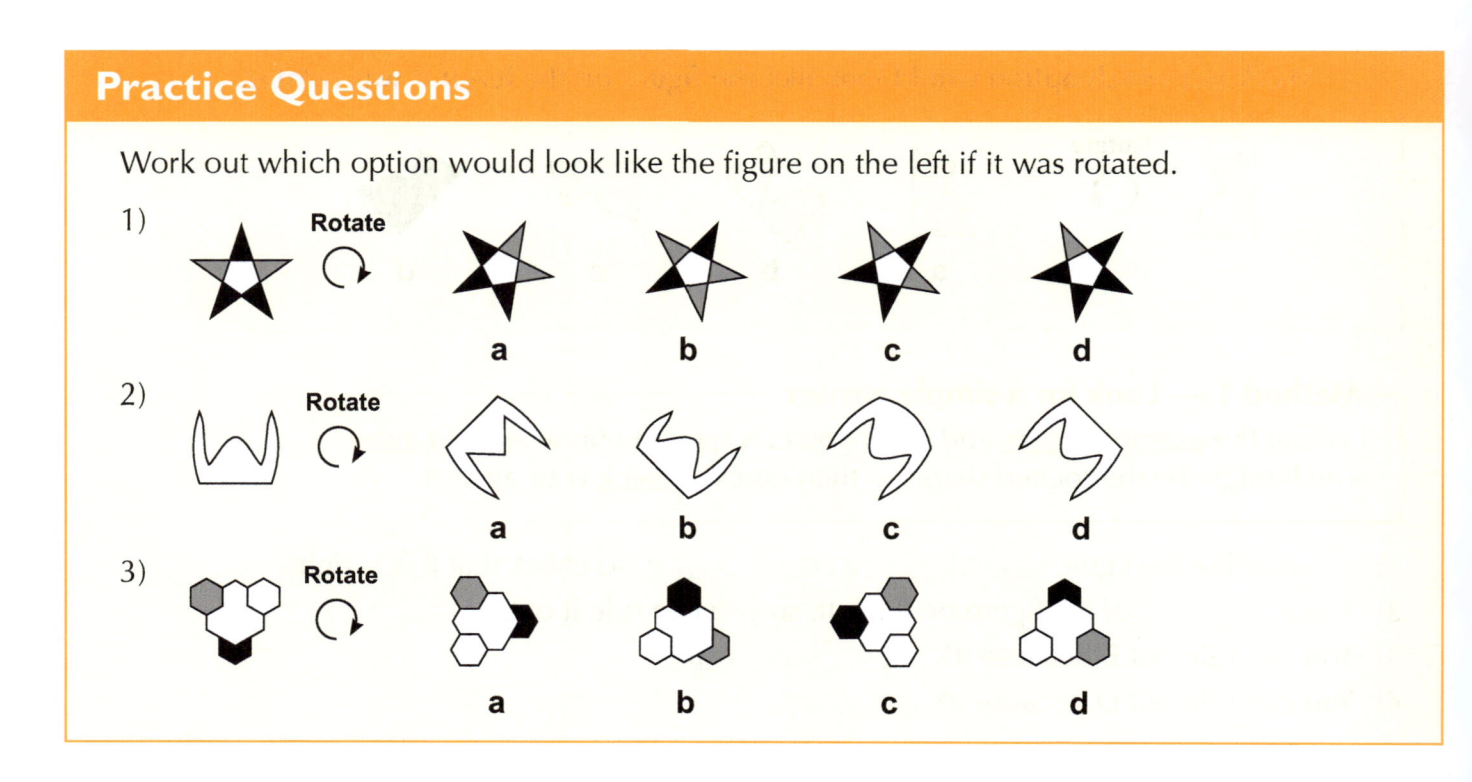

Practice Questions

Work out which option would look like the figure on the left if it was rotated.

1) Rotate
   a   b   c   d

2) Rotate
   a   b   c   d

3) Rotate
   a   b   c   d

Question Types — Rotation and Reflection

Reflect the Figure

The idea behind reflection questions is pretty simple — you've got to reflect a figure over a line. Unfortunately, some of the actual questions aren't as simple...

Warm-Up Activity

1. Find another person to play this game with you. Each of you should draw a shape on a separate piece of paper.
2. Swap shapes and have a race to see who can draw the reflection of the shape fastest. Then check with a mirror to see how accurate the reflected shapes are. The winner is the person who draws an accurate reflection fastest.

Find the Option that's a Reflection of the Example Figure

1) You'll be shown an example figure next to a line and four or five options.
2) You have to pick the option that's a reflection of the example figure over the line.

Try to spot an Obvious Answer first

The first thing to do is imagine what the example figure would look like if it was reflected.

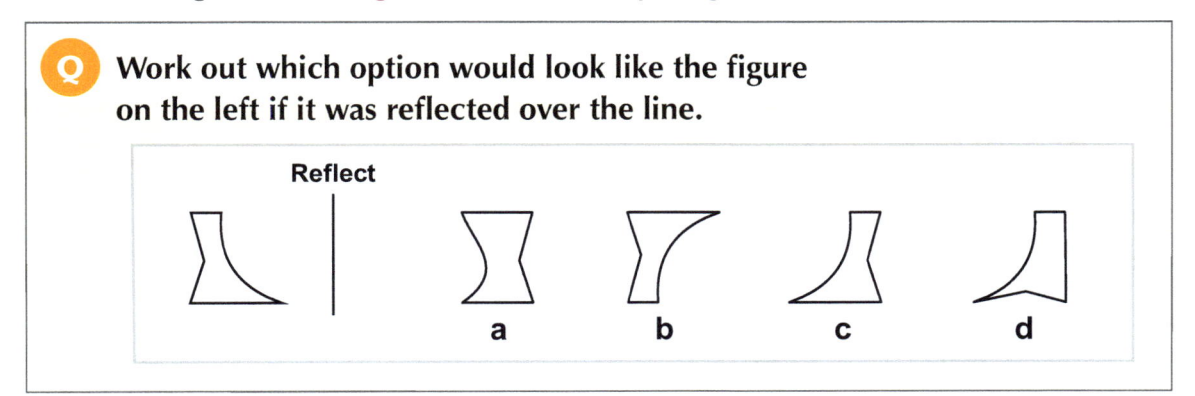

Q Work out which option would look like the figure on the left if it was reflected over the line.

Method 1 — Imagine reflecting the example shape
1) Look for a distinctive feature on the example figure.
2) Rule out any options that don't have this feature.
3) Keep looking for other features and ruling out options which don't have them.

1) The right-hand side of the example image curves down from the top and out to the right. Its reflection will have the opposite curve on its left-hand side. The only options that are like this are C and D, so you can rule out A and B.
2) The left-hand side of the example figure has two lines bent inwards. The answer must have these lines on the right-hand side, so the correct answer must be C.

Sometimes the Figures can be quite Complicated

The figure can be more complicated than a simple shape — it might be two or more shapes together.

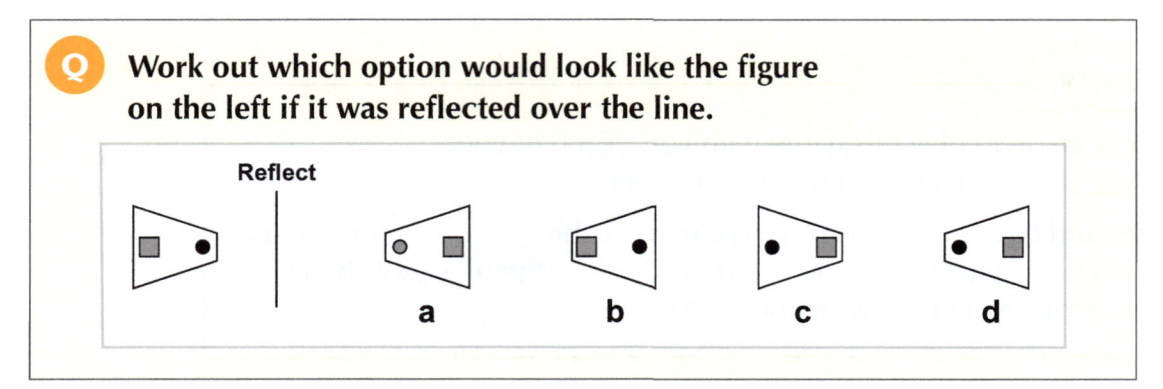

Q Work out which option would look like the figure on the left if it was reflected over the line.

Method 2 — Look at each part of the figure separately

1) First look at the largest shape (or outline) and work out what its reflection should look like — rule out any answers that don't look like this.

2) Then look at any smaller shapes and rule out options where they're not reflected correctly.

1) In C, the large white shape has not been reflected, so you can rule it out.

2) Look at the positions of the dot and the square. Their positions have not been reflected in B, so you can rule it out.

3) In the figure on the left, the circle is black, but in A it is grey. This means you can rule out A, and the answer must be D.

Practice Questions

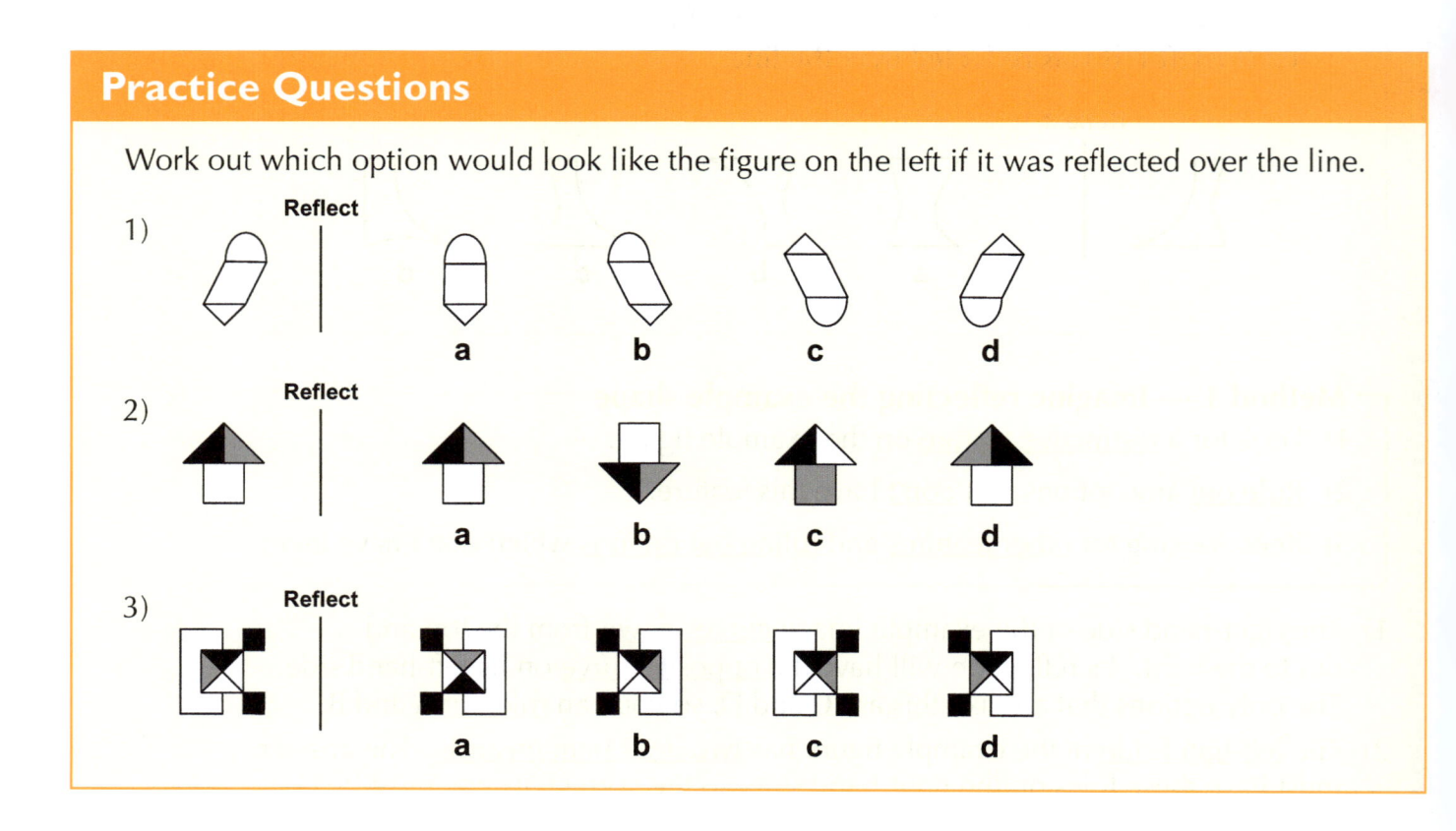

Work out which option would look like the figure on the left if it was reflected over the line.

1)

2)

3)

Question Types — Rotation and Reflection

Question Types — 3D Shapes and Folding

3D Shapes and Folding

There's loads going on in this section. First, there are some question types that involve 3D shapes. After that, it's on to questions that involve imagining you're folding and unfolding shapes.

You might need to Rotate 3D shapes

These questions are all about working out what 3D shapes would look like if they were rotated, put together, taken apart or moved.

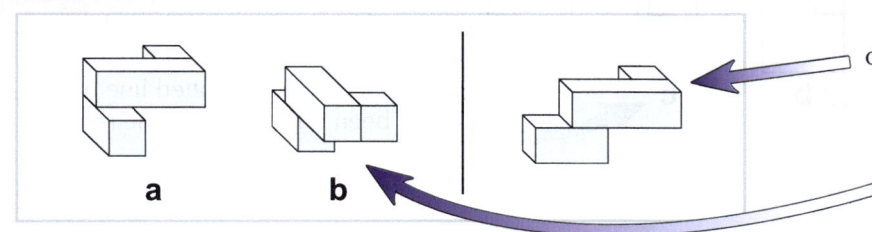

3D Rotation

You've got to work out which option is the same as the figure on the right, after rotation.

The answer is B. It has been rotated 90 degrees left-to-right.

3D Building Blocks

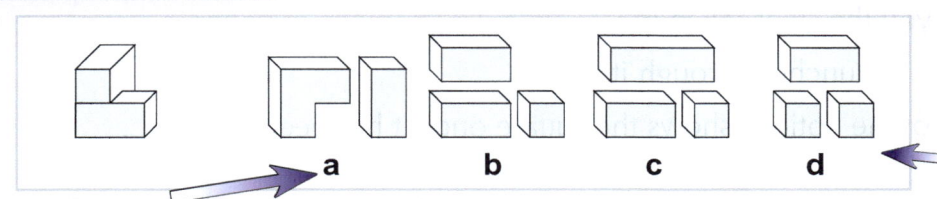

You've got to work out which of the sets of blocks on the right can be rearranged to make the figure on the left.

The answer is A — there are only two blocks in the figure on the left.

You might need to Switch between 2D and 3D

Here you'll need to imagine what 3D shapes look like in 2D and what 2D shapes look like in 3D.

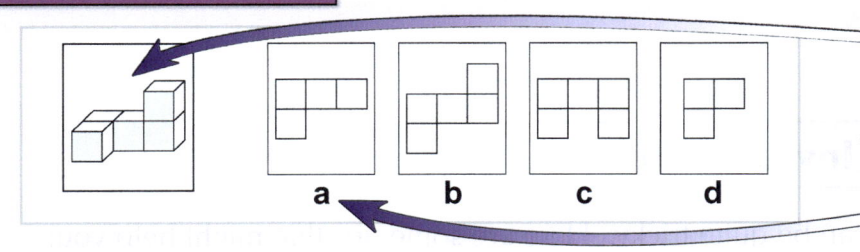

2D Views of 3D Shapes

You've got to work out what the figure on the left looks like if viewed directly from above.

There will be four blocks visible from above, which means that A is the answer.

Cubes and Nets

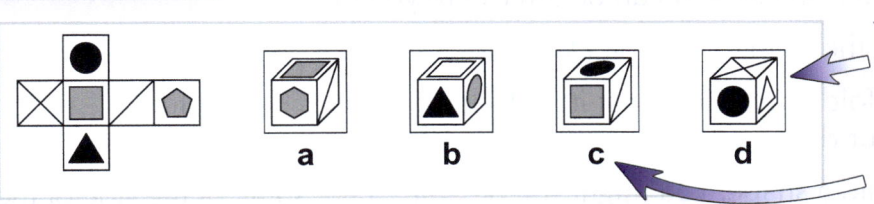

You've got to work out which of the cubes can be made from the net on the left.

Options A, B and D all have shapes that don't appear on the net — the answer is C.

You might need to imagine **Folding** a shape **Along** a **Line**

1) These questions are about working out what a shape looks like after it's been folded.
2) You'll be shown a shape that has a dotted fold line drawn across it.
3) You'll be asked which option shows that shape after it has been folded along the fold line.

Fold Along the Line

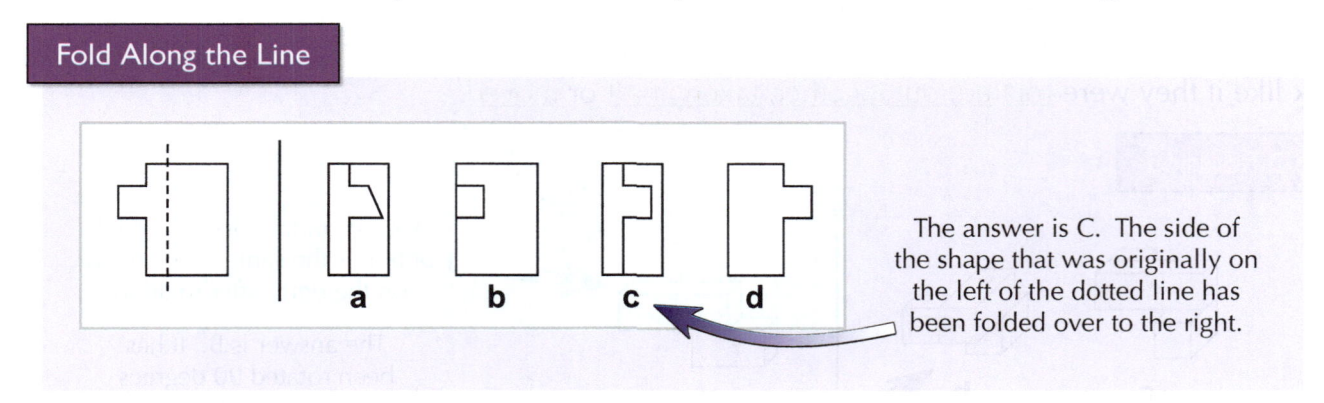

The answer is C. The side of the shape that was originally on the left of the dotted line has been folded over to the right.

You might need to imagine **Unfolding** a **Square**

1) These questions show you the steps taken to fold up a square piece of paper.
2) The paper then has a hole punched through it.
3) You'll be asked which of the options shows the square once it has been unfolded.

Fold and Punch

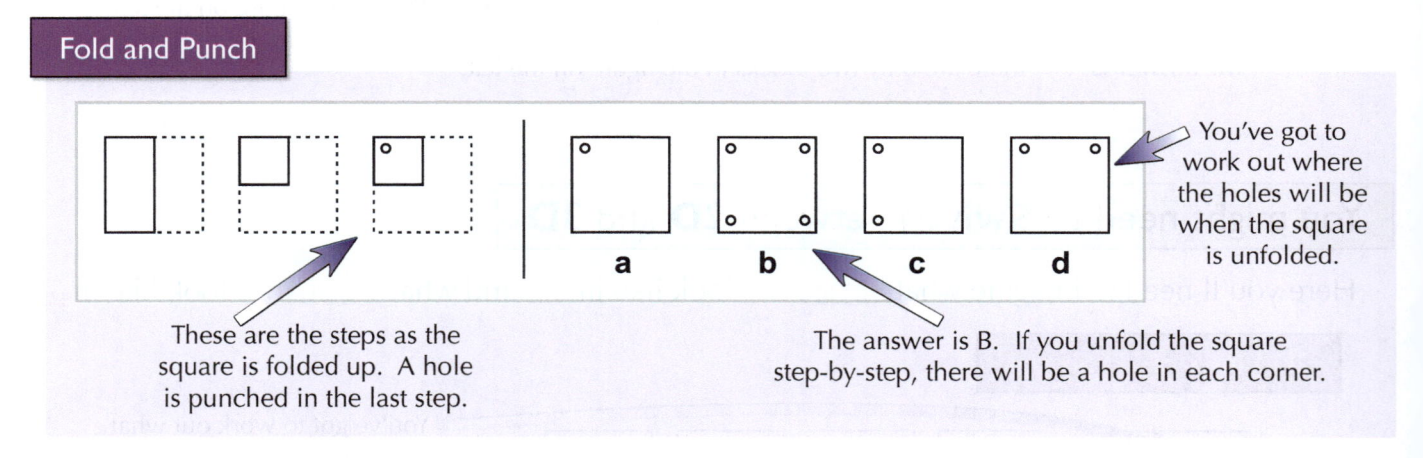

These are the steps as the square is folded up. A hole is punched in the last step.

The answer is B. If you unfold the square step-by-step, there will be a hole in each corner.

You've got to work out where the holes will be when the square is unfolded.

Doing your own **Folding Investigations** will help

Questions that involve folding can be quite tricky. Here are some tips that might help you:

1) Try drawing some big shapes on a piece of paper and then cut them out.
   Draw a fold line across each shape — it can be anywhere you like.
2) See if you can draw what the shape will look like when it's been folded along your line.
3) Fold the shape along the fold line to see what it looks like when it's been folded.
   Compare the shape to your drawing to see how well they match.
4) Don't forget, when you fold a shape, you might still be able to see some of the side of the shape that hasn't been folded. Don't just think about the shape of the bit that you've folded.

Question Types — 3D Shapes and Folding

3D Rotation

You've already had a go at rotating things in 2D — it's time to add another dimension. These questions are all about spotting 3D shapes after they've been rotated in 3D space.

Warm-Up Activity

Look around the room you're in and pick four objects, such as a mug or a lamp. Draw a quick sketch of them from where you're sitting. Then draw another sketch of what you think the back of the objects might look like. Look at the backs of the objects to see how close you were.

Work out which Option is the Same as the Example Figure

1) For a 3D Rotation question you'll be given several different 3D shapes as answer options. You'll also be given another shape that is exactly the same as one of the answer options, except it has been rotated.
2) It can be rotated in any direction and by any amount. You have to try to imagine what the figure would look like if it was rotated, and match it to one of the answer options.

Work out which Types of Block are used

Sometimes you can find the answer just by looking at the blocks that make up the shape.

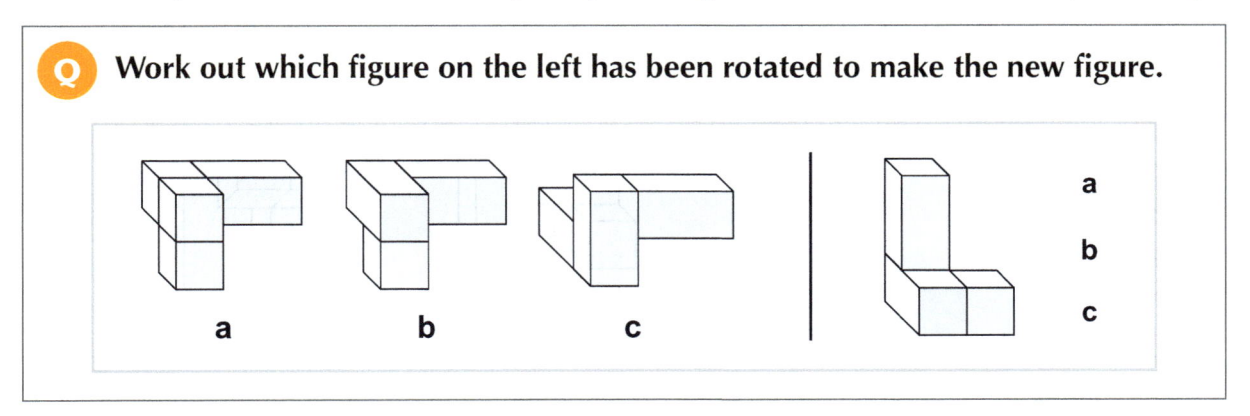

Q Work out which figure on the left has been rotated to make the new figure.

Method 1 — Think about the number and type of blocks

1) Count the number of blocks used to make the figure. Rule out any options with a different number of blocks.
2) Look at the types of block and rule out any options with the wrong blocks.

1) In this example, the figure has three blocks. A has four blocks, so you can rule it out.
2) The example figure has a cube as well as two longer blocks. C has three blocks, but they are all the same length, so you can rule it out. The answer must be B.

Question Types — 3D Shapes and Folding

Look at the **Shape** of the **Figure**

Sometimes one part of a 3D shape is easy to recognise.

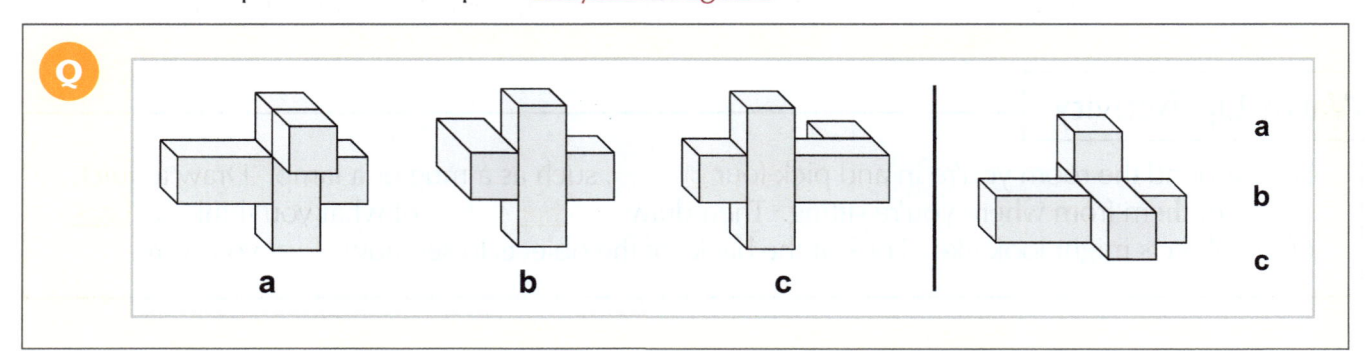

Method 2 — Look for shapes that stand out

1) Look at each part of the figure and try to spot an overall shape that stands out. This could be something like an L-shape, an S-shape or a cross.
2) See if you can spot this shape in any of the answer options. Then compare the rest of the figure to the answer option to make sure that it all matches up.

1) The base of the figure on the right is a cross with one arm longer than the others. B has a cross, but all the arms are the same length, so you can rule it out.
2) In C, there is a cube attached to the long arm of the cross, instead of one of the short arms, so you can rule it out. The answer must be A.

Practice Questions

Work out which figure at the top has been rotated to make the new figure. Circle its letter.

1) a b c d

2) a b c d

3) a b c d

4) a b c d

Question Types — 3D Shapes and Folding

3D Building Blocks

These questions are all about imagining what groups of blocks would look like if you put them together to make a larger 3D shape. If you've got some building blocks, now's the time to use them.

Warm-Up Activity

Look around the room you're in. Pick out a few objects, such as a computer, a chair or a chest of drawers. Try to draw them using as few shapes as possible, such as cubes and cuboids. Show your drawings to another person and see if they can recognise the objects.

You have to Build the figure using Blocks

1) You'll be given a 3D figure that is made up of several blocks — usually between two and four. You'll also be given some sets of separate blocks.
2) You have to work out which set of blocks can be put together to make the 3D figure.
3) The blocks in the sets can be rotated by any amount and in any direction to make the figure. You'll have to imagine what the blocks would look like if they were rotated and combined.

Look for Blocks that are Obvious

In some questions, it is clear which blocks make up the figure.

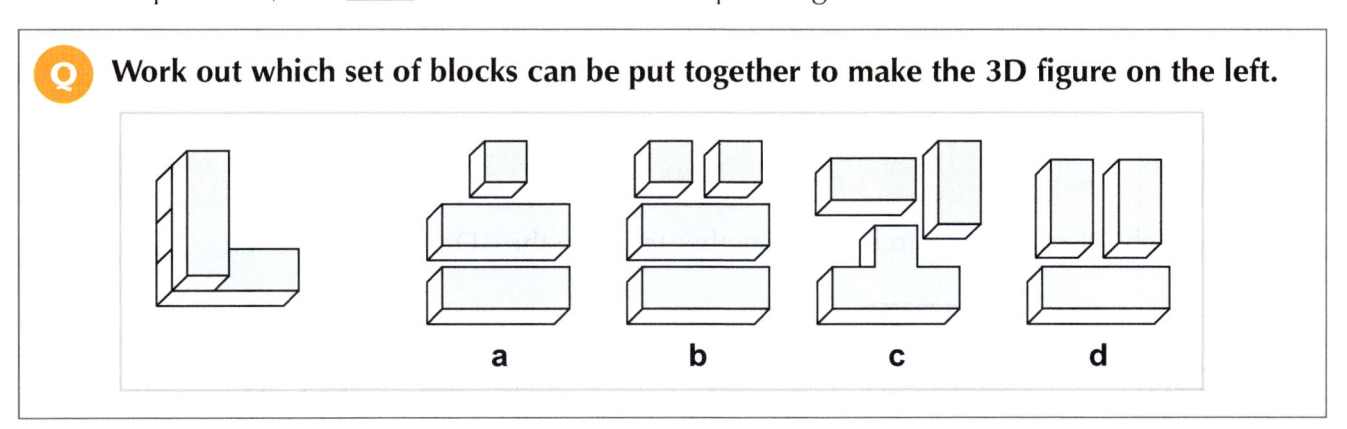

Q Work out which set of blocks can be put together to make the 3D figure on the left.

a   b   c   d

Method 1 — Rule out options with the wrong blocks

1) Look to see whether there are any types of block that are definitely part of the figure.
2) Rule out all the options that don't have that block.

The front of the figure is a good place to start — it's usually easier to tell which blocks are being used.

1) In this example, the front block must be three cubes long. C doesn't have this block, so you can rule it out.
2) The block at the bottom of the figure at the back also must be a block three cubes long. This rules out D because it only has one block three cubes long.
3) There are two cubes in the figure, so the answer is B.

Question Types — 3D Shapes and Folding

Parts of some blocks could be **Hidden**

If part of the figure is hidden then it's not always easy to tell what blocks make up the figure.

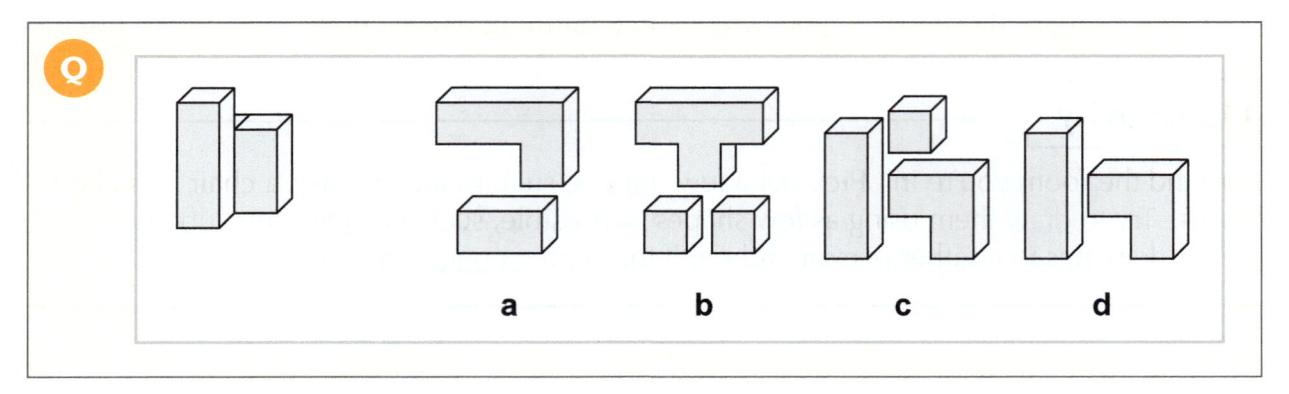

Q

  a   b   c   d

In this example, you can't tell straight away what the front-left block is — it could be a block three cubes long, an L-shaped block or a T-shaped block.

Method 2 — Think about what each block could be

1) Look at any blocks that you're unsure about and work out what they could be.
2) For each possibility, work out what the other blocks in the set would need to be.

1) If the front-left block was an L-shape three blocks high, A would be the only option. The block on the right of the figure could be the block at the bottom of set A, but there is still another block in the middle of the figure at the back. A can't be the answer.
2) The front-left block could also be a T-shape. However, B is the only option with a T-shape and none of the other blocks in B could be the block on the right of the figure. B can be ruled out.
3) This means that the front-left block must be a block three cubes long. There are at least two other blocks needed to make the figure. D doesn't have enough blocks — the answer is C.

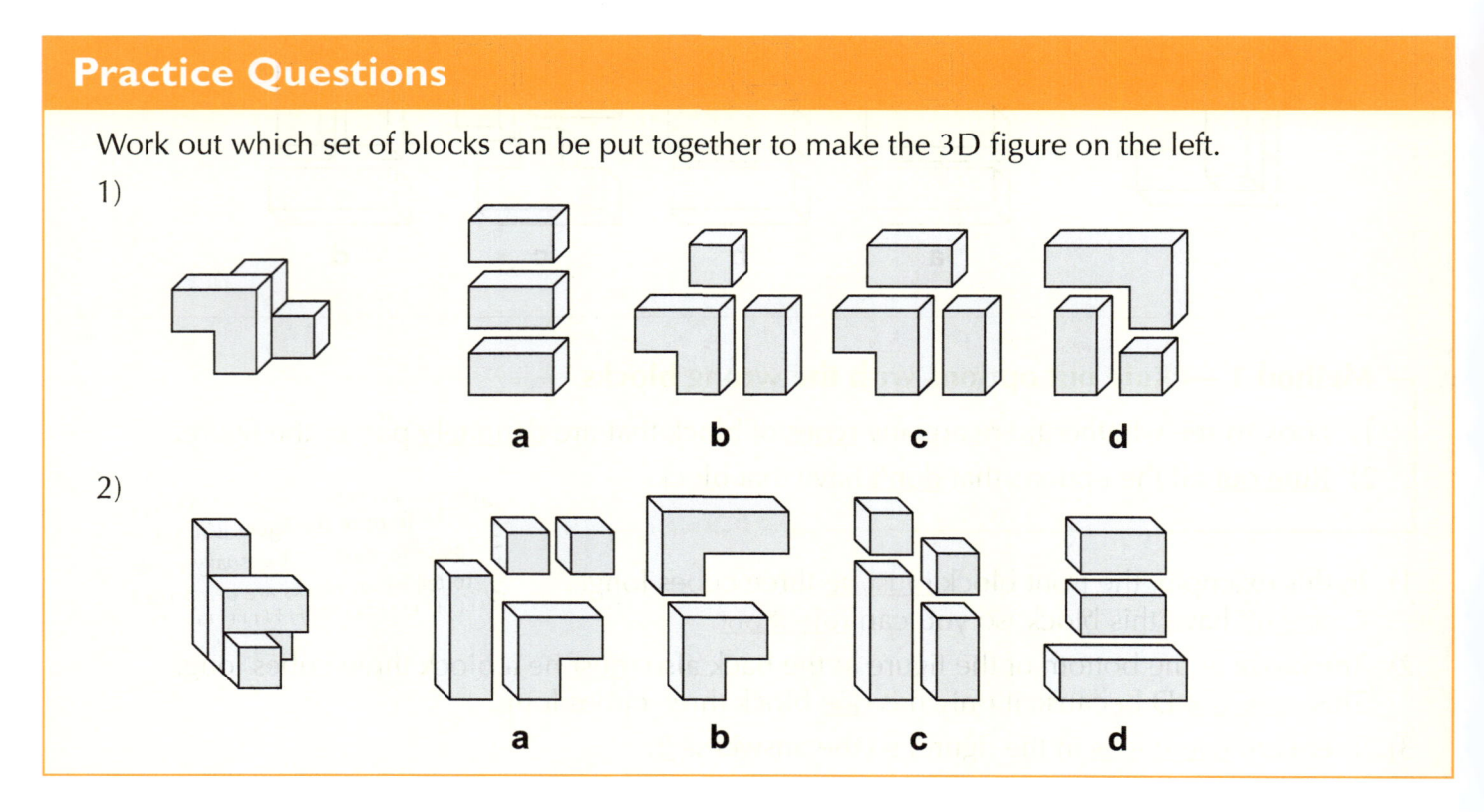

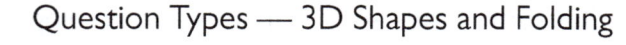

Practice Questions

Work out which set of blocks can be put together to make the 3D figure on the left.

1)

  a   b   c   d

2)

  a   b   c   d

Question Types — 3D Shapes and Folding

2D Views of 3D Shapes

Imagine looking at a cube from directly above. It will just look like a square on its own.
Now imagine you've got a group of cubes together and you're looking at them from above...

Warm-Up Activity

Look around the room you're in and pick a few objects, such as a table, a cup or a chair. Try to draw what they would look like when viewed from above. Have a look at the objects from above and see how close your drawings were.

You have to Imagine a 3D shape in 2D

1) You'll be given a 3D shape made up of several cubes, and some 2D shapes made up of squares.
2) You need to imagine what the 3D shape looks like when viewed from directly above.
3) Then you need to choose the option which matches this 2D view.

Work out how many Blocks you can see from Above

Counting the number of blocks that are visible from above is a good place to start.

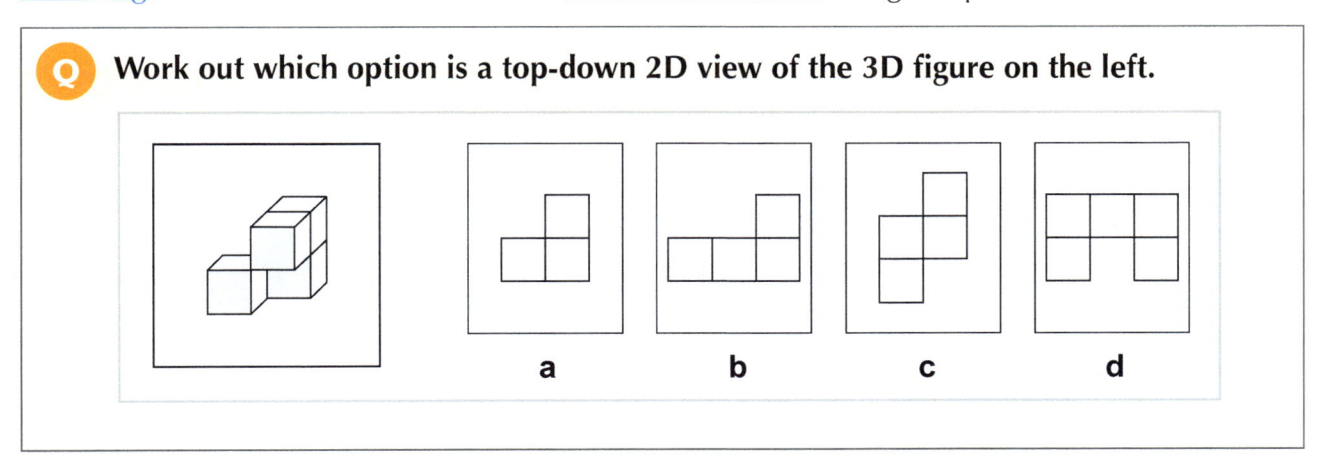

Q Work out which option is a top-down 2D view of the 3D figure on the left.

a b c d

Method 1 — Think about the number of blocks

1) Count the number of blocks that can be seen from directly above.
2) Rule out any options with a different number of blocks.

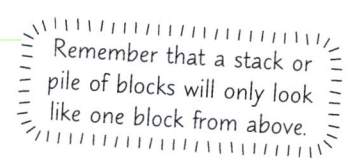

Remember that a stack or pile of blocks will only look like one block from above.

In this example, the cube at the back of the shape on the bottom-right won't be seen from above, because it's part of a stack. Only three blocks can be seen from above — the answer is A.

Tips and Tricks for 2D Views of 3D Shapes questions

If you're allowed to write on the test paper, put a small cross or dot on the top face of each block that can be seen from above. Then count the marks you have made.

Question Types — 3D Shapes and Folding

Look at the Positions of the Blocks

Sometimes there will be a gap in the 3D shape that will make a gap in the 2D view.

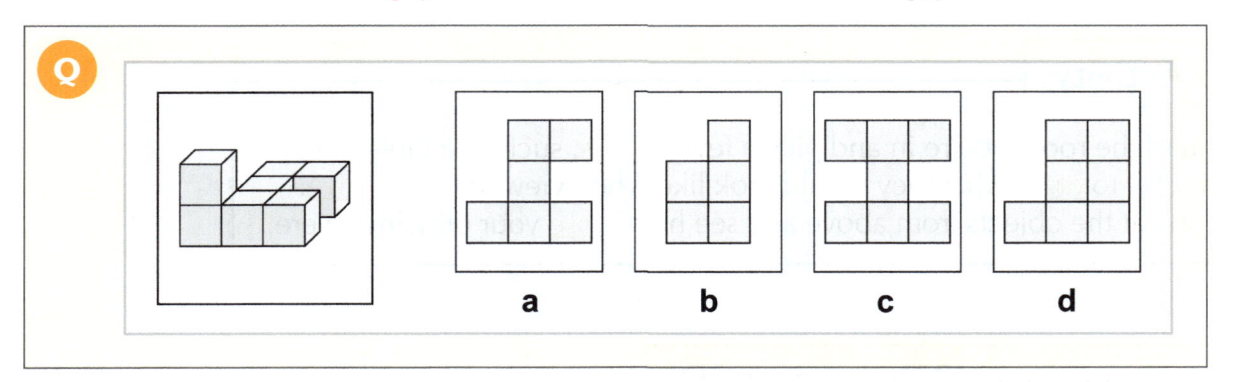

Q

      a   b   c   d

Method 2 — Look at the positions of the visible blocks

1) Count the blocks at the front of the figure and look for any gaps between them.
2) Rule out any options that don't look like this.
3) Do the same with the other sides of the figure until you find the right answer.

1) There are three blocks visible at the front of the figure — this rules out B.
2) On the right-hand side, there is a gap between the front and back blocks — this rules out D.
3) There are two blocks at the back of the figure — this rules out C. The answer is A.

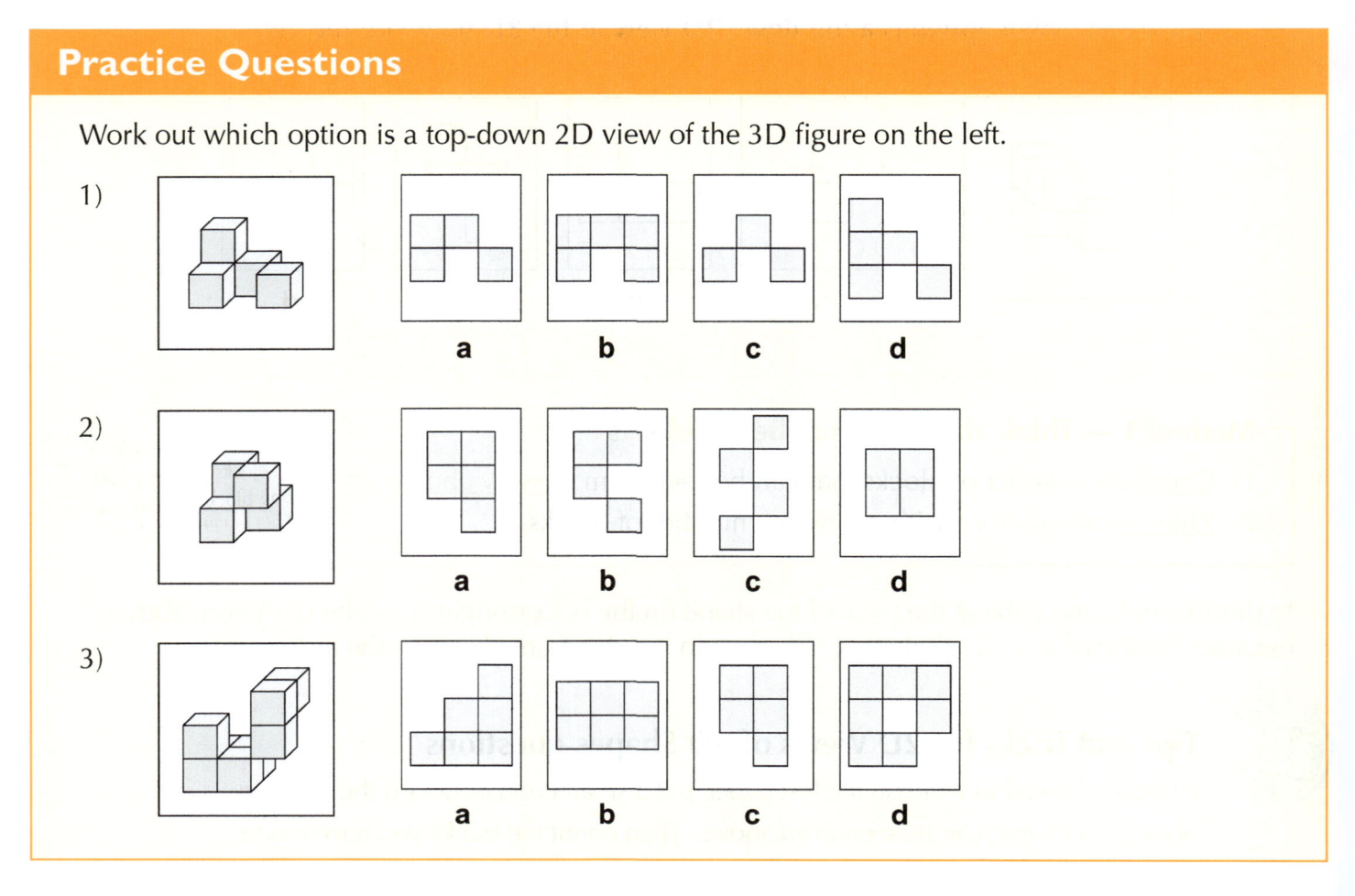

Practice Questions

Work out which option is a top-down 2D view of the 3D figure on the left.

1)   a   b   c   d

2)   a   b   c   d

3)   a   b   c   d

Question Types — 3D Shapes and Folding

Cubes and Nets

This section's about turning 2D nets into 3D cubes. If you find these questions tricky, you could cut out some cube nets, draw the figures on them and fold them into cubes to see how they fit together.

Warm-Up Activity

Trace the net on the right and draw it on a new piece of paper. Cut out the net and draw a shape or design in pencil on each square. Fold it to make a cube and see how the shapes fit together.

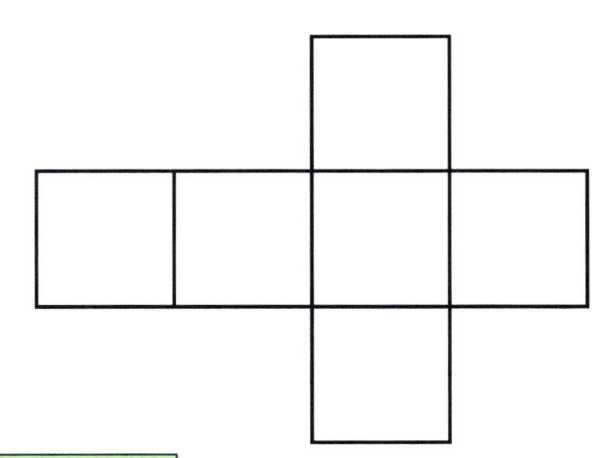

You have to work out which Cube matches the Net

1) For Cubes and Nets questions, you'll be given a net for a cube along with several cubes.
2) You'll have to work out which of the cubes can be made from the folded net.

Rule Out options that are Wrong

Sometimes you can rule out options without having to imagine folding the net.

Q Work out which of the four cubes can be made from the net. Circle its letter.

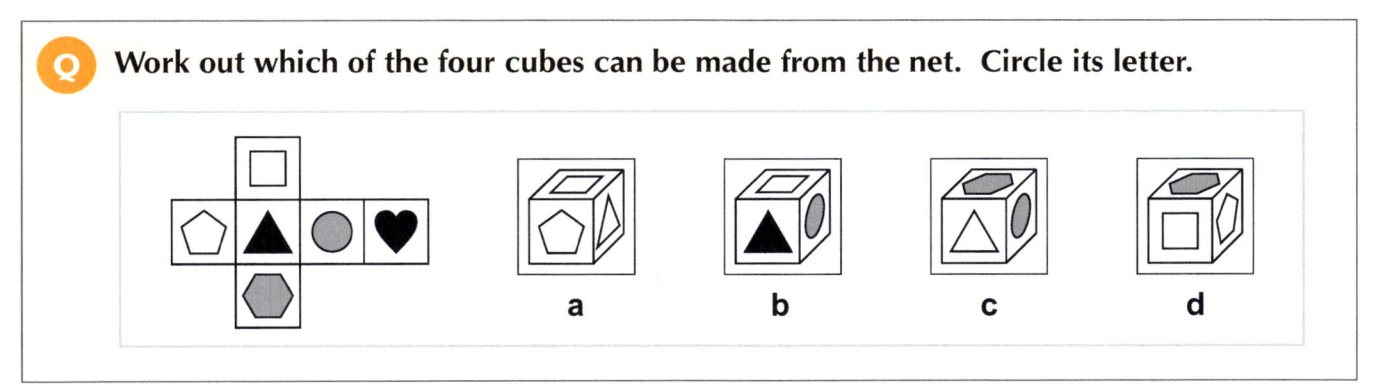

Method 1 — Compare each cube with the net

1) Rule out options with shapes that aren't on the net.
2) Faces on opposite sides of the cube can't be seen at the same time — rule out any options where opposite faces appear together on the cube. You can tell when faces on the net will be opposite each other on the cube because they're separated by one other face.

1) In the example, you can rule out A and C because they both have a white triangle that isn't on the net.
2) The opposite faces of the cube in this example are the pentagon and the circle, the triangle and the heart, and the square and the hexagon. D has a square and a hexagon next to each other, so you can rule it out. The answer is B.

Question Types — 3D Shapes and Folding

Some options might be Harder to Rule Out

Even if the shapes can all appear on the cube, they might be on the wrong side or rotated incorrectly.

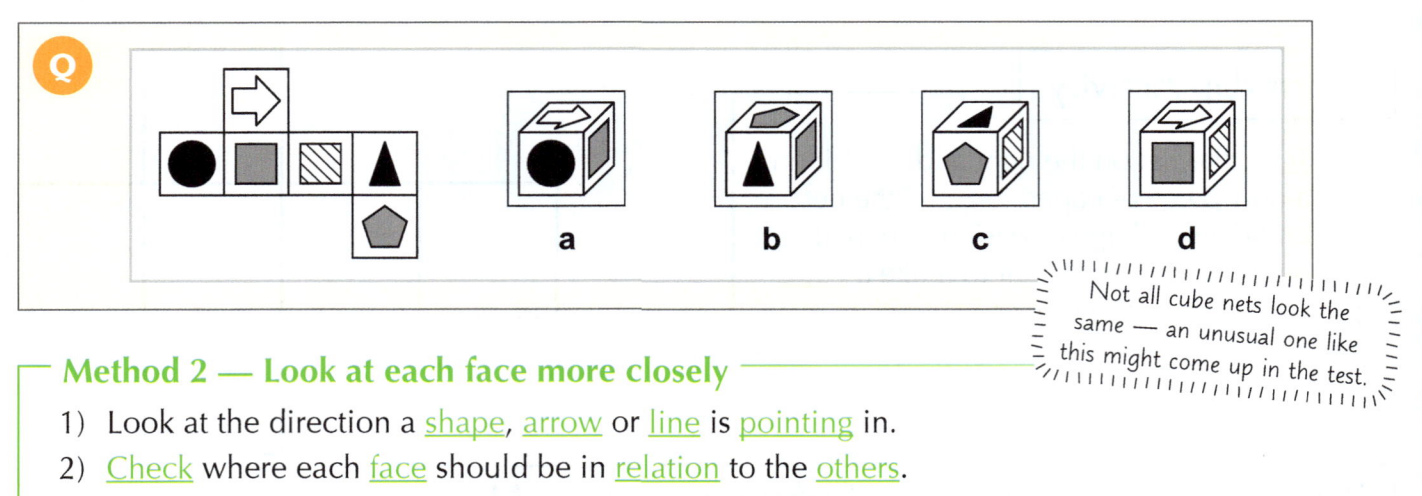

Method 2 — Look at each face more closely
1) Look at the direction a shape, arrow or line is pointing in.
2) Check where each face should be in relation to the others.

Not all cube nets look the same — an unusual one like this might come up in the test.

1) You can rule out B because the black triangle and the grey square must be on opposite sides of the cube, so they can't appear together.
2) In A, all the faces are in the right place, but the arrow shouldn't be pointing at the grey square — you can rule it out.
3) The cube faces in C can all appear together. However, if you folded the net so the triangle was at the top and the pentagon was at the front, the hatched square should be on the left, not the right. You can rule out C, so the answer must be D.

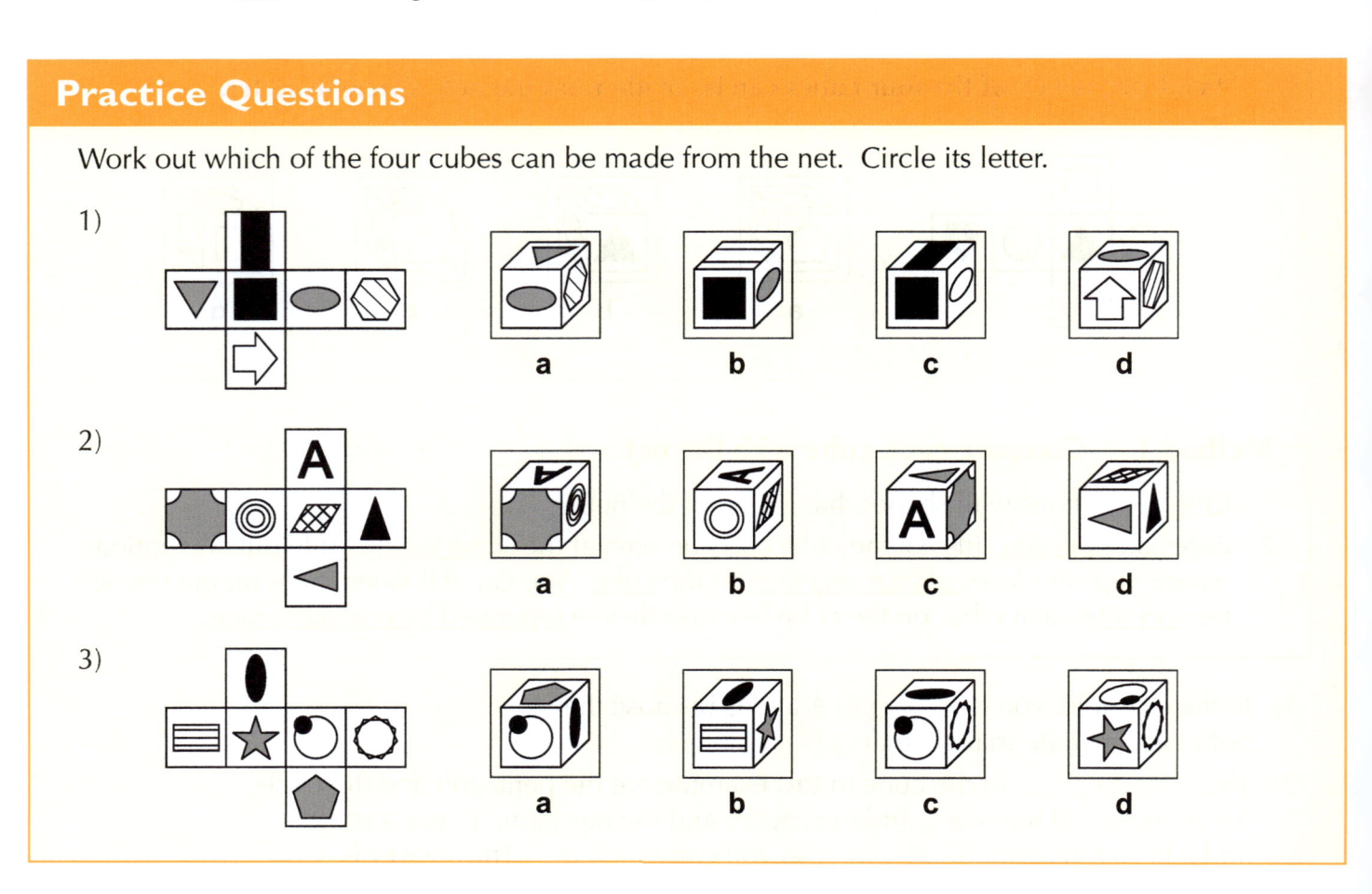

Practice Questions

Work out which of the four cubes can be made from the net. Circle its letter.

1)

2)

3)

Question Types — 3D Shapes and Folding

Folding

In these questions, you have to imagine folding or unfolding a shape. If you get to grips with this now, you won't be folding up your 11+ paper into teeny tiny squares in a panic...

Warm-Up Activity

Find another person to play this game with you. Each of you should fold a piece of paper in half. You should both then draw a large shape on your paper (try not to make it too simple or too complicated). With the paper still folded, cut the shape out. This will give two identical shapes.

Each person should fold one of their shapes once, and then show it to the other person. The other person should then try to draw where the fold line should go on the copy of the shape.

Each person can then unfold their shape to see how accurate the other person's line drawing was.

Rule Out options that are Wrong

There are a few ways that options might be wrong. There might be something wrong with its shape, the fold line might have moved or the shape might have broken apart along the fold line.

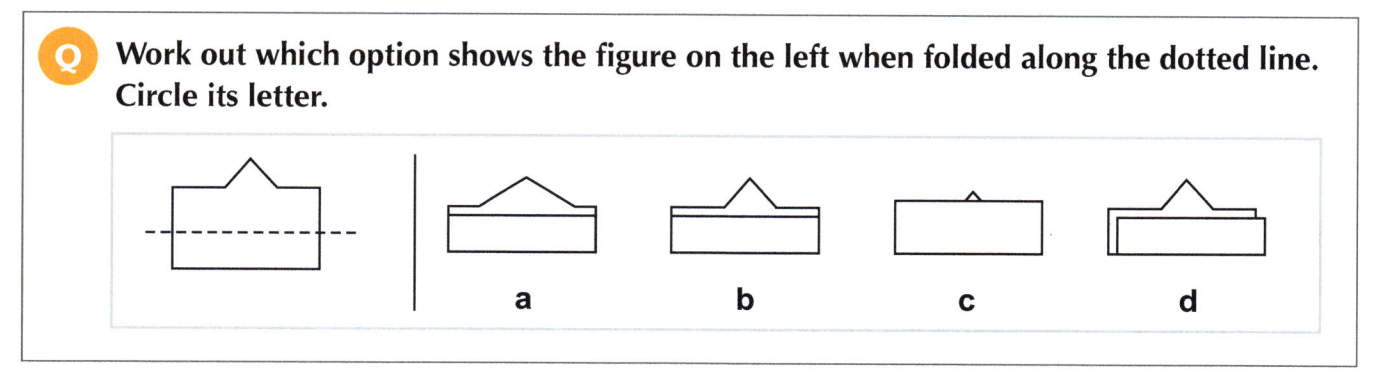

Q Work out which option shows the figure on the left when folded along the dotted line. Circle its letter.

Method 1 — Compare the shapes of the figures
1) Rule out options where the figure has changed shape.
2) Look carefully at the shape of the figure on both sides of the fold line.
3) You should also look out for places where you should be able to see a part of the shape, but it is missing in the option.

In the example, you can rule out A because the part of the shape that was originally above the fold line has changed shape. The triangular part at the top is too wide.

Method 2 — Check the fold line
1) Rule out options where the fold line has moved.
2) The figure will still have the right shape, but it might be folded in the wrong place.
3) Also, look out for places where the shape has broken apart where the fold line was.

1) In the example, you can rule out C because the fold line has moved.
   A bigger part of the shape has been folded and less of the triangular part is showing.
2) You can rule out D because the shape has broken apart where the fold line was.
3) This means the answer is B. The bottom part of the figure has been folded upwards.

Question Types — 3D Shapes and Folding

Being able to **Unfold** a shape in your head is **Important**

As well as having to fold shapes, you might also get questions which ask you to unfold shapes.

Q A square is folded and then a hole is punched, as shown on the left.
Work out which option shows the square when unfolded. Circle its letter.

a   b   c   d

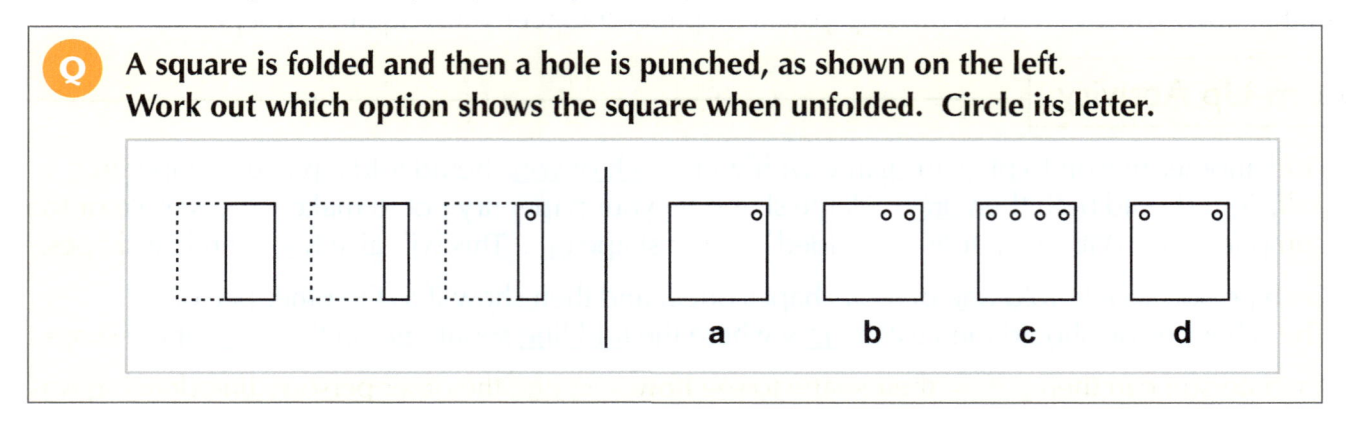

Method — Unfold the shape step-by-step

1) Work backwards from the final folded shape. Imagine unfolding each fold one at a time.
2) At each step, work out where there will be new holes.
3) Depending on where the fold was, there might not be new holes each time.

1) Unfold the final fold that was made in the question.
You'll then have two holes.

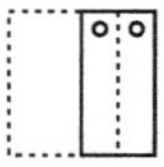

2) Unfold the first fold. This will reveal another two holes.
So the answer is C.

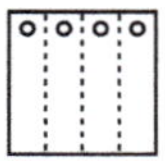

Practice Questions

Work out which option shows the figure on the left when folded along the dotted line. Circle its letter.

1)

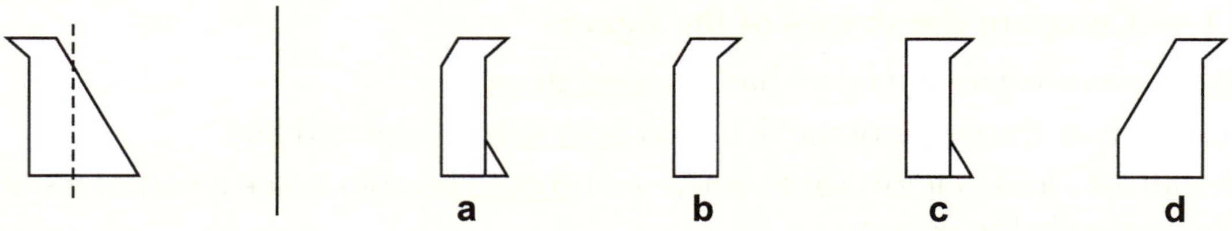

a   b   c   d

A square is folded and then a hole is punched, as shown on the left.
Work out which option shows the square when unfolded. Circle its letter.

2)

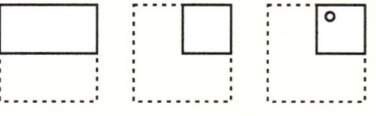

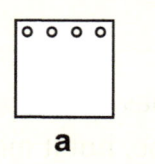

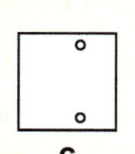

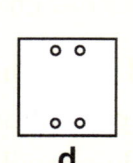

a   b   c   d

3)

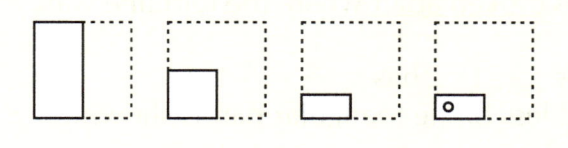

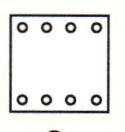

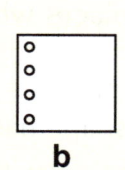

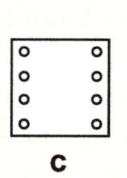

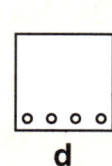

a   b   c   d

Question Types — 3D Shapes and Folding

Glossary

Rotation and Reflection

Rotation is when a shape is turned clockwise or anticlockwise from its starting point.

Example shape | 90 degrees clockwise rotation | 45 degrees anticlockwise rotation | 180 degrees rotation

The hands on a clock move clockwise:
Anticlockwise is the opposite direction:

Reflection is when something is mirrored over a line (this line might be invisible).

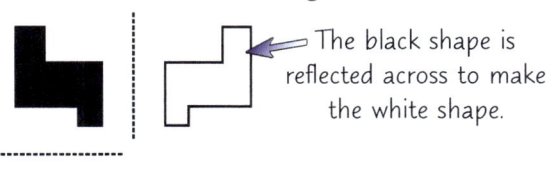

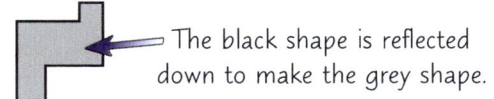

The black shape is reflected across to make the white shape.

The black shape is reflected down to make the grey shape.

3D Rotation

There are three planes that a 3D shape can be rotated in.

1. 90 degrees towards you, top-to-bottom
   90 degrees away from you, top-to-bottom

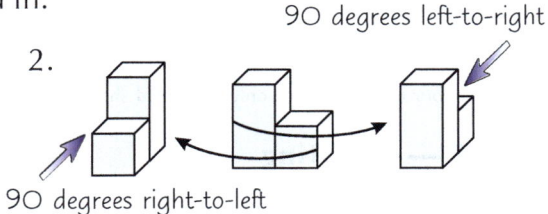

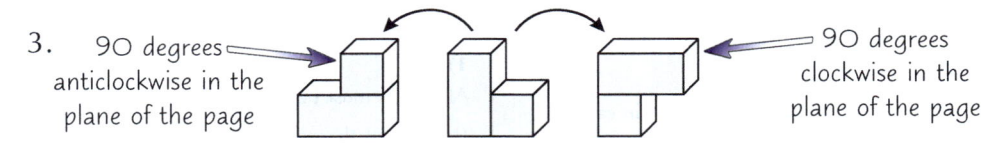

2. 90 degrees left-to-right
   90 degrees right-to-left

3. 90 degrees anticlockwise in the plane of the page
   90 degrees clockwise in the plane of the page

Other Terms

Line Types: Thin, Thick, Dashed, Dotted, Curved

Shading Types: Black, Grey, White, Two types of hatching, Cross-hatched, Spotted

Layering — when a shape is in front of or behind another shape, or where two or more shapes overlap each other.

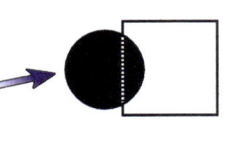

The circle is in front of the square. The right-hand shape is a cut-out shape made from the overlap of the two shapes.

Line of Symmetry — a line which splits a shape into halves that are reflections of each other.

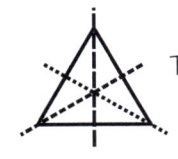

This triangle has three lines of symmetry.

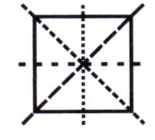

A square has four lines of symmetry.

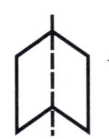

This shape has one line of symmetry.

Glossary

Answers

Spotting Patterns

Page 7 — Shapes
Practice Questions

1) D
All the other shapes have five sides.
(Counting the sides of each of the shapes shows you that D is the only shape that has a different number of sides from the rest, with four sides instead of five.)

2) D
All figures must be triangles.
(Counting the sides of the example figures shows you that they both have three sides. D is the only figure that also has three sides.)

3) A
The shape in the next series square always has one less side than the shape in the series square before it.
(Counting the sides of each of the shapes shows you that the number of sides of the shapes goes in the order: seven, six, five. This means that the next shape must have four sides. A is the only four-sided shape.)

Page 9 — Counting
Practice Questions

1) B
All the other figures have the same number of lines crossing the outline of the shape as the number of black dots inside the shape.
(Keeping track of the number of small lines and dots in each figure shows you that there is a connection between the two types of object. B is the only figure which does not share this connection — it has two lines and three dots.)

2) B
In all figures, the number of black shapes must be one less than the number of sides of the outer shape.
(Counting the number of sides of the large shape and the number of black shapes in the example figures shows you that there is a connection between the two — the first example has four sides and three black shapes, the second example has five sides and four black shapes. B is the only figure where the number of black shapes is one less than the number of sides of the large shape, with four sides and three black shapes.)

3) B
An extra black dot turns grey in each series square.
(Keeping track of the number of black dots and grey dots in each figure shows you how many black and grey dots the next figure should have. The number of grey dots goes in the order: one, two, three. The next figure must have four grey dots. The number of black dots goes in the order: five, four, three. The next figure must have two black dots. B is the only figure which has four grey dots and two black dots.)

Page 11 — Pointing
Practice Questions

1) D
In all other figures, the arrow is pointing away from a four-sided shape and towards a circle.
(If the arrows in all the figures don't share a common direction you should check whether the arrows all point towards or away from a common shape. D is the only figure in which the arrow points towards a four-sided shape and away from a circle.)

2) A
The arrow switches between going clockwise and anticlockwise. The length of the arrow decreases in each series square.
(You can see that the arrow gets shorter in each square, so you don't have to work out how much smaller it is getting to realise that the missing square must have the shortest arrow. This means you are left with a choice between A and D. The arrow swaps between going clockwise and anticlockwise. The arrow in the third square is going clockwise, so you know that the arrow in the missing square must be going anticlockwise. This leaves you with A as the answer.)

3) D
All arrowheads must point right.
(By looking at the example figures, you can see that they both point in the same direction. D is the only figure which also points right.)

Page 14 — Shading and Line Types
Practice Questions

1) D
All shapes must be hatched and have a dashed outline.
(Looking at the example figures, you can see that they are both hatched. This leaves you with a choice between A and D. The two example figures also have the same sort of dashed outline. A has a solid outline, which leaves you with D as the answer.)

2) A
An extra two squares turn black in each series square.
(The number of black squares goes in the order: two, four, six. The missing figure must have eight black squares. A is the only figure with eight black squares, so it must be the answer. You could also work out the answer by looking at the white squares, which go in the order: fourteen, twelve, ten. The missing figure must have eight white squares, which also gives you A.)

3) E
All the other figures are made up of four lines.
(By counting the lines for each figure you can see that E has five lines, while the rest only have four. You could also look at the number of gaps in each figure's outline to work out the answer.)

Page 17 — Position

Warm-Up Activity
Tangram Square

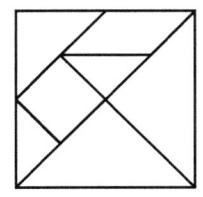

Practice Questions

1) B

The heart moves round the shape one side at a time in an anticlockwise direction. The arrow moves up the middle of the hexagon.

(By working out the movement of both the small shapes, you know that the next square must have the arrow at the very top of the hexagon, and the heart on the right-hand side of the hexagon at the bottom. B is the only option that fits both of these descriptions.)

2) C

In all other figures, the shapes are in the same positions — in C the circle and the raindrop have swapped places.

(Checking the position of each shape in turn will help you spot any differences.)

3) A

In each series square, a shape is removed in a clockwise direction.

(Counting the shapes in each square shows you that there is one less shape each time, going in the order: six, five, four. The missing figure must have three shapes. This leaves you with a choice between A and C. Because the shapes are removed in a clockwise direction the cross should be the next shape to disappear. In C the star has been removed, which leaves you with A as the answer.)

Page 19 — Order

Practice Questions

1) D

Working clockwise, the shapes in all the other figures go in the order: ellipse, star, trapezium.

(Picking the same small shape on the outline as a starting point and then counting round in the same direction for each of the figures will help you work out if the shapes are in an order. The order is the same for all the figures, apart from D, which has the order: ellipse, trapezium, star.)

2) A

Each shape moves one place to the left in each series square.

(The shapes in all the examples have the same order: circle, square, hexagon (going from left to right). When the shape on the left-hand side can't move any further left, it appears again on the right-hand side in the next series square. A is the only figure where all the shapes are in the right order and the right positions: circle, square, hexagon (from left to right). Because there are only three shapes and three positions, it looks identical to the figure in the first square.)

Page 22 — Rotation

Practice Questions

1) A

The figure has been rotated 135 degrees clockwise. Options B and D are rotated reflections. Option C is the wrong shape.

(To help you see the rotation, take one part of the figure and rotate the page so that this one part faces the same way in each figure. If you rotate all the options so the longest side of the shape is on the bottom, you will notice that in B and D the cross shape is on the right instead of the left. They have been reflected. This leaves you with a choice between A and C. There is no cross shape in figure C, which leaves you with A as the answer.)

2) A

The black quarter-circle rotates 45 degrees anticlockwise around the centre of each series square. The diamond rotates 90 degrees anticlockwise in each series square.

(To help you see the rotation of the quarter-circle, pick one of the straight edges of the quarter-circle and see how it has rotated in the next square. The quarter-circle in the missing square must be a 45 degree anticlockwise rotation of the quarter-circle in the third square, so it must be on the left-hand side of the square. This leaves you with a choice between A and D. Picking either the grey or the white half of the diamond and following it round will help you work out how the diamond is rotating. The next square must have the diamond rotated so that the grey half is on the right, which leaves you with A as the answer.)

3) C

Ignoring the hatching, the right-hand shape in all figures must be a 90 degree clockwise rotation of the left-hand shape. The hatching in the right-hand shape must be a 45 degree anticlockwise rotation of the hatching in the left-hand shape.

(This question shows why you should always double check how the hatching of a shape changes. If you thought that both the shape and the hatching rotated 90 degrees together, you would get D as the answer. If you work out the rotation of the right-hand shape, you are left with a choice of C and D. C is the only option that has the correct hatching rotation. Rotating the page might help you work out how the shape and hatching should look in the right-hand shape.)

Page 25 — Reflection

Practice Questions

1) B

In all other figures the bottom shape is a downwards reflection of the top shape.

(Imagining a horizontal line dividing each of the figures in half might make the reflection easier to see. The black shading of the bottom shape in figure B is the wrong way round for it to be a reflection — the bottom shape is actually a 180 degree rotation of the top shape.)

2) C

In options A and B, the black circle is in the wrong place in relation to the arrow. Option D is a 180 degree rotation.

(In this question you have to imagine that there is a mirror along the 'reflect' line. The circle is at the top on the side closest to the mirror, so in the reflection the circle will also be at the top on the closest side (the left-hand side). This leaves you with a choice between B and C. The arrow is at the bottom, so in the reflection the arrow will also be at the bottom. This leaves you with C as the answer.)

Answers

3) **C**

The shape rotates 90 degrees anticlockwise and moves to the next side of the series square in an anticlockwise direction. After rotation, the shape reflects back on itself over its longest side.

(This is quite a difficult question because the mirror line changes position in each square. To make it easier to see the mirror line you could rotate the page so that the shape is always at the bottom of each square.)

Page 28 — Layering
Practice Questions

1) **E**

In all other figures, the hatched shape is a 90 degree clockwise rotation of the shape made by the overlap of the two white shapes.

(The hatched shape in figure E is not the same shape as the overlap of the two white shapes, no matter how it is rotated — it's actually the shape left when you take the overlap away from the triangle.)

2) **B**

All figures must have a black shape at the front, and a white shape at the back.

(Looking at the example figures, they both have shapes layered in the same order from front to back: black, grey, white. A has both the white shape and the black shape at the front. C has a grey shape at the front and D has a grey shape at the back. This means that B is the only option that has the colours on the right layers.)

3) **D**

Working from front to back, all other figures go in the order: pentagon, ellipse, arrow.

(You can check the order by picking the same shape to start with in all figures, and counting from that shape back. In D, the arrow and the ellipse have swapped places, giving the order: pentagon, arrow, ellipse.)

Question Types

Page 32 — Odd One Out
Practice Questions

1) **B**

All of the other figures have a solid outline.

(The figures are all the same colour and all the shapes are different, so neither of these things help you find the odd one out. A and C are symmetrical, but B and D don't have any lines of symmetry, so symmetry doesn't help you either. They all have solid outlines except B, which has a dashed outline, so this must be the answer.)

2) **D**

In all other figures, the ends of the curved lines point away from the ellipse. In D, they point towards the ellipse.

(All five of the figures are identical except for rotation, colour and the direction the curved lines point in. Figures A, C and D have the same colour scheme as each other. Figures B and E have the same colour scheme as each other, so colour doesn't help you find the odd one out. Figures A, B and D are rotated the same way, and figures C and E are rotated the other way, so rotation doesn't help you either. Only D has its curved lines pointing in a different direction from the other four, so that must be the odd one out.)

3) **A**

In all other figures, two of the arcs have their gaps facing the black dot, and one has its gap facing the edge of the hexagon.

(All the figures are white hexagons with black dots in the centre, and they all have three arcs, so none of these things are helpful when you're looking for the odd one out. In figures A, B and D there's one arc at the top and two at the bottom. In figures C and E, there are two at the top and one at the bottom — this doesn't help you find the odd one out either. Only A has arcs pointing in a different direction to the rest, so this must be the answer.)

Page 35 — Find The Figure Like The Others
Practice Questions

1) **C**

All figures must have a small white shape inside a larger grey shape.

(The example figures both have two shapes, and one of the shapes is inside the other one. This leaves options B and C. In both the example shapes the inside shape is white. Figure B has a grey inside shape, which means the answer must be C.)

2) **D**

In all figures, the number of black dots must be the same as the number of sides on the shape with the smallest number of sides.

(The first example figure has three dots, one shape with three sides and one with four sides. The second example figure has five dots, one shape with five sides, and one with six sides. The third has four dots, one shape with four sides, and one with six sides. D is the only option that shares the same connection as the example figures, with four dots, one shape with four sides, and one with five sides.)

3) **B**

In all figures, the arrow must go clockwise around the circle. The beginning and the end of the arrow must line up with the beginning and the end of the black part of the circle.

(In all three of the example figures, the arrow goes clockwise around the circle. Figures C and E have arrows going anticlockwise and D has two arrowheads. This leaves options A and B, so you've got to look back at the example figures to see what else they've got in common. In all the example figures the arrow lines up with the beginning and end of the black part of the circle. The arrow in figure A doesn't line up with the black part of the circle. This means that B is the answer.)

Page 39 — Complete The Pair
Practice Questions

1) **D**

The figure is rotated 90 degrees clockwise and the hatching becomes cross-hatched.

(In the first pair, the ellipse and the arrow both rotate 90 degrees clockwise. The hatching inside the ellipse changes from being hatched to cross-hatched. In the second pair, the triangles both rotate 90 degrees clockwise. The hatching inside the smaller triangle changes from being hatched to cross-hatched. The same thing must happen to the third pair — the rectangle and the trapezium both rotate 90 degrees clockwise, so that the shortest side of the trapezium is at the bottom. This rules out A and C. The hatching inside the rectangle becomes cross-hatched. This rules out B, so the answer is D.)

2) B

The lines that form the sides of the large shape get longer so they cross each other. The outline of the small shape changes from solid to dotted.

(In the first pair, the lines that make up the pentagon's sides get longer so they cross over. The small circle's outline changes from solid to dotted. In the second pair, the lines that make up the hexagon's sides get longer so they cross over. The small diamond's outline changes from solid to dotted. This means that in the third pair, the lines that make up the square's sides get longer, which rules out A and D. The small triangle's outline changes from solid to dotted, which rules out C, so the answer is B.)

3) D

The larger white shape rotates 90 degrees and the outline of the grey shape changes from solid to dotted. The star turns black.

(In the first pair, the ellipse rotates 90 degrees. The outline of the diamond changes from solid to dotted and the star turns black. In the second pair, the hexagon rotates 90 degrees. The outline of the circle changes from solid to dotted and the star turns black. In the third pair, the rectangle rotates 90 degrees, which rules out A and B. The outline of the grey circle changes from solid to dotted, which rules out C, which means the answer must be D.)

Page 42 — Complete The Series
Practice Questions

1) A

In each series square, another section of the pentagon becomes hatched in a clockwise direction. The line between the old hatched section and the new hatched section disappears. The hatching rotates 90 degrees in each series square.

(Each large shape in the series is a pentagon, which rules out B. The lines between the sections disappear when the sections become hatched, which rules out D. The hatching from the fourth square rotates 90 degrees, which rules out C, so the answer must be A.)

2) C

In each series square, one black triangle gets replaced by one white circle.

(Counting the number of each type of shape in the series squares is a good place to start. The number of black triangles goes down by one in each series square: four, three, two. There must be one black triangle in the fourth series square, which rules out B and D. The number of white circles goes up by one in each series square: one, two, three. There must be four white circles in the fourth series square, which rules out A, so C must be the answer.)

3) B

In each series square, the circle moves clockwise around the four points of the star. The gap in the star's outline moves one side clockwise.

(Working backwards along the series (from right to left), you can see the circle and the gap in the star's outline moving anticlockwise around the star. The next position the circle will be in is on the left-hand point of the star, which rules out A and C. The next position the gap will be in is on the right-hand side of the top point. This rules out D, so B must be the answer.)

Page 47 — Complete The Grid
Practice Questions

1) C

Working from top to bottom, the shape rotates 90 degrees anticlockwise in each grid square.

(The shapes in each column are all the same, which rules out A, B and E. Working from bottom to top, the shape rotates 90 degrees clockwise in each column, so C is the answer.)

2) E

Each pattern inside the squares only appears once in each row and column. Along each row, the grid square on the right contains both of the right-angled lines from the left-hand grid square and the middle grid square.

(The only pattern which hasn't already appeared in the bottom row and the middle column is the pattern made of eight triangles, which leaves options C and E. Looking along the first two rows, the right-hand grid square has two right-angled lines and the other two squares only have one. The two in the right-hand square are in the same positions as the two in the left-hand and middle squares. On the bottom row, the two lines are in the top right-hand and bottom left-hand corners. The left-hand square has a right-angled line in the top right, so the answer must have one in the bottom left-hand corner. This rules out option C, so the answer must be E.)

3) B

Going clockwise around the hexagonal grid, the shaded corner of the triangle moves one corner clockwise. The colour of the shading alternates between black and grey.

(The shading of the triangle changes position in each hexagon. Starting from the top hexagon and going clockwise, the shading is in the position: top, bottom-right, bottom-left. The missing triangle should have the shading at the top of the triangle, which rules out A and C. The shading alternates between black and grey. On either side of the missing hexagon, the shading is black, so the shading in the answer must be grey. This rules out D, so B is the answer. You could also find the answer by noticing that the figure is the same in opposite hexagons, but with the shading changed.)

Page 50 — Rotate The Figure
Practice Questions

1) C

The figure has been rotated 45 degrees clockwise. The other figures are all shaded incorrectly.

(There are two grey points on the star, which rules out B and D. The two grey points are not next to each other, which rules out A. The answer is C.)

2) D

The figure has been rotated 225 degrees clockwise (or 135 degrees anticlockwise). The other figures are all the wrong shape.

(The middle part of the figure should be a curve, which rules out A. The two 'arms' on either side of the figure should be the same length, which rules out B. There should be one straight line in the figure, which rules out C, so the answer is D.)

3) D

The figure has been rotated 180 degrees. A is a rotated reflection. B and C are both layered incorrectly.

(The small grey and white hexagons should both be in front of the large white hexagon, and the black hexagon should be behind it. This rules out B and C. If A and D were rotated so the black hexagon was at the bottom, the grey hexagon should be on the left-hand side. This shows that A is a rotated reflection, so the answer must be D.)

Page 52 — Reflect The Figure
Practice Questions

1) B
Figure A is the wrong shape. C is a rotated reflection. D is a 180 degree rotation.

(The semicircle is at the top of the figure, so in a reflection across it will stay at the top of the figure, which rules out C and D. The white parallelogram has become a white rectangle in A, so B is the answer.)

2) D
Figure A is identical to the figure on the left. B is a reflected rotation. C has the wrong shading.

(In the figure, the grey triangle is closest to the line of reflection, so the answer will also have the grey triangle closest to the line of reflection. This rules out A, B and C, so D is the answer.)

3) B
Figures A and D have the wrong shading. In C, the large white rectangle and the small black squares have not been reflected.

(The large white rectangle is on the left-hand side of the figure on the left, so the answer will have the white rectangle on the right-hand side. This rules out C. The triangle at the top is black, and will also be black in the reflection, which rules out A. The triangle furthest from the line of reflection is grey, so the answer will also have the grey triangle furthest from the line of reflection, which rules out D, so the answer is B.)

Page 56 — 3D Rotation
Practice Questions

1) A
The figure has been rotated 90 degrees anticlockwise in the plane of the page, then 180 degrees left-to-right.

(You could also look at the types of blocks to find the answer. The figure in this question has one cube and two blocks which are two cubes long. B, C and D all have different sets of blocks, so A must be the answer.)

2) D
The figure has been rotated 90 degrees clockwise in the plane of the page. It has then been rotated 180 degrees left-to-right.

(The figure in this question has two blocks two cubes long that make an L-shape. There is a block attached to the middle of the L-shape which could be one block two cubes long, or a cube attached to another cube. D is the only option which matches this shape, so it must be the answer.)

3) B
The figure has been rotated 180 degrees in the plane of the page. It has then been rotated 90 degrees towards you top-to-bottom.

(The figure in this question has a C-shape at the top. This matches the shape of B and C, which rules out A and D. The cube sticking out at the bottom of the figure is attached to a block two cubes long, which rules out C, so B is the answer.)

4) C
The figure has been rotated 180 degrees in the plane of the page. It has then been rotated 90 degrees towards you top-to-bottom.

(The figure in this question has a C-shape at the top, which rules out A and D. The cube sticking out at the bottom of the figure is attached to another cube, which rules out B, so C is the answer.)

Page 58 — 3D Building Blocks
Practice Questions

1) B
The block on the right of set B moves behind the block on the left of the set. The block at the top of set B moves to the right at the back of the figure.

(The block at the front of the figure must be a short L-shaped block, which rules out A and D. The back of the figure must be made of either three cubes, an L-shaped block, or one cube and a block two cubes long. C doesn't have any of those possibilities, so B is the answer.)

2) A
One of the cubes at the top of set A moves in front of the L-shaped block to become the front of the figure on the left. The block on the left of set A moves behind the L-shaped block and the other cube moves to the right of this block to become the back right-hand part of the figure.

(The front two blocks must be a cube and a short L-shaped block. B, C and D do not have these blocks, so the answer is A.)

Page 60 — 2D Views Of 3D Shapes
Practice Questions

1) A
There should be four blocks visible from above, which rules out B, C and D.

(You can also find the answer to this question by looking at the positions of the blocks — there should be two blocks on the left of the figure, which rules out C and D. There should be two blocks along the back of the figure, which rules out B.)

2) D
There should be two blocks at the front of the figure, which rules out A, B and C.

(You could start this question by counting the number of blocks visible from above. There are four, which rules out A. But then you would also have to look at the positions of the blocks to work out whether the answer is B, C or D.)

3) B

There should be six blocks visible from above, which rules out C and D. There should be two blocks on the left-hand side of the figure, which rules out A. The answer must be B.

(Questions where some blocks are floating can be tricky. The stack of two floating blocks on the right of the figure touches the row of blocks at the bottom. This tells you that if they were on the ground, the cubes would be next to each other and the answer should have a row of three squares at the front of the figure.)

Page 62 — Cubes And Nets
Practice Questions

1) D

The grey ellipse and the grey triangle should be on opposite sides, which rules out A. There is no face with just two white lines, so this rules out B. There is no face with a white ellipse, which rules out C, so D is the answer.

2) A

There is no face on the net with just two circles, which rules out B. The letter 'A' and the grey triangle should be on opposite sides, which rules out C. The black triangle does not point to the cross-hatched parallelogram on the net, which rules out D.

3) C

The grey pentagon and the black ellipse should be on opposite sides, which rules out A. The longest lengths of the black ellipse and the hatched rectangle should be parallel to each other, which rules out B. The five-pointed star and the eleven-pointed star should be on opposite sides, which rules out D, so C is the answer.

Page 64 — Folding
Practice Questions

1) A

Option B is ruled out because the part of the figure originally to the right of the fold line should still be visible. Option C is ruled out because the part of the figure that has been folded is the wrong shape. Option D is ruled out because the fold line has moved.

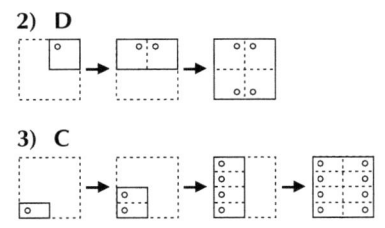

2) D

3) C

Index

0-9

2D Views of 3D Shapes 53, 59, 60
3D Building Blocks 53, 57, 58
3D Rotation 53, 55, 56
3D shapes 2, 53, 55-62

A

addition 8, 9, 13
angles 6, 20
anticlockwise 11, 19, 20
arrows 10, 11
arrow-style lines 10

C

clockwise 11, 19, 20
common movements 16
Complete the Grid 36, 43-47
Complete the Pair 36-39
Complete the Series 36, 40-42
counting 4, 8, 9
Cubes and Nets 53, 61, 62

D

differences 15, 29-35
directions 10, 20

E

elements 4
equal numbers 9

F

Find the Figure Like the Others 29, 33-35
Fold Along the Line 54, 63
Fold and Punch 54, 64
folding 54, 63, 64
fractions 13

G

grids 2, 36, 43-47

H

hatching 12, 22, 24
hexagonal grids 46, 47
hexagons 5

L

layering 4, 26-28
lengths 6
line types and styles 4, 14

M

maths 8, 13
mirror lines 23, 25, 48
mirrors 7, 23, 48
missing figures 40-47
movement 16, 18, 19, 28
multiple choice 1

N

Non-Verbal Reasoning 2, 3

O

Odd One Out 29-32, 35
order 4, 18, 19, 27, 28
outlines 26
overlaps 26, 27

P

pairs 2, 36-39
parallelograms 24
patterns 45, 47
pointing 4, 10, 11
position 4, 15-17, 26-28

Q

quadrilaterals 5
question types 2, 29-62

R

rectangles 5
Reflect the Figure 48, 51, 52
reflection 4, 23-25, 48, 51, 52
reflection and rotation 2, 25
Rotate the Figure 48-50
rotation 4, 20-22, 25, 48-50
rule questions 35

S

sequences and series 2, 5, 36, 40-42, 44
shading 4, 12-14, 19, 28
shapes 4-7
sides 5, 6, 14
similarities and differences 2, 15, 29-35
size 6
spinners 10
square grids 43-46
standard answer 1
subtraction 8, 9, 13
symmetry 7

T

tangrams 3, 15
triangles 5, 6
types of grid pattern 45, 47

What is the 11+?

It can be tricky to find reliable information about the 11+ and how to prepare for it. This page covers the basics — what the 11+ test is and how it works.

The 11+ is a selective test

Most secondary schools in the UK are comprehensive — they're non-selective and accept children of all abilities. But in some areas, selective state secondary schools (grammar schools) still exist. These schools select their pupils based on academic ability.

The 11+ test is used to determine if a child is suitable for grammar school. It's also used for entry to some independent schools. Children usually sit the test in the first term of their last year at primary school. Some schools select pupils based just on the 11+ test results, but others look at other factors, e.g. whether you live close to the school, or if you have other children at the school.

The format of the test varies

The exact format of the 11+ test varies depending on the school or Local Authority (LA) you're applying to, but the topics that can be tested are:

> **Verbal Reasoning** — problem-solving and logic using words, letters, etc.
> **Non-Verbal Reasoning** — problem-solving using pictures and symbols.
> **Maths** — often at the same level as the SATs, but it may be more challenging.
> **English** — reading comprehension, grammar and sometimes a writing task.

Your child's 11+ test could include any combination of these subjects. In tests set by the CEM, the Verbal Reasoning sections cover many of the English elements.

The tests may be multiple choice (MC), standard answer (SA) or a mixture of the two.

> - **Multiple choice** — there may be a separate answer sheet. There's usually a choice of four or five options for each answer, and the answers are often computer-marked.
> - **Standard answer** — there are spaces on the question paper for the answers.

There are two main test providers

11+ tests used around the country aren't all written by the same organisation, so it's important to find out what kind of test your child will be sitting, and the types of question they'll have to do.

> - **GL Assessment** are one of the main test providers. They produce tests to order. This means that a Verbal Reasoning test for one school won't be exactly the same style as one for another, even though they're both set by GL Assessment.
> - **Centre for Evaluation and Monitoring (CEM)** tests are used in some areas. They're designed to test natural ability and aim to minimise the effects of tutoring, so it's difficult to work out what will be in the test from year to year.

Some schools write their own test papers.

See the next page for more information on the test and the application process.

Entering the Test

The 11+ varies greatly, depending on the area you live in. This page will give you an introduction to how it works, but it's no substitute for doing your own research.

The 11+ is different in each area

In some areas, every child who wants to go to grammar school sits the same test which is organised by the LA. Your child might be entered for this test automatically. In other areas, you'll need to apply to each grammar school individually, and your child will sit a separate test for each school you've applied to.

Even in areas where the LA handles entry for the majority of grammar schools, there may still be some schools which must be applied for separately. These schools may also set a separate test.

You'll need to research each school you're going to apply to for up-to-date information on admissions. Schools must publish their admissions criteria online, or you can get information from your local authority about the schools in your area. Check the application deadlines carefully for each school you apply to, as they can vary quite widely.

For up-to-date information on the format of the 11+ in your area, go to
cgpbooks.co.uk/11plus

Some tests are organised by LAs

In some areas, the LA organises the 11+ test for most or all of the grammar schools in the region. You can get information about the content and date of the test, deadlines and other admission criteria from the LA's website, or by contacting them directly.

If your child is in a state primary school within the area covered by the LA of your chosen school, you might find that the 11+ is arranged through the school, unless you choose to opt out.

If you live outside of the local authority area, or your child is at an independent prep school, contact the LA to find out how to enter your child for the test.

Some tests are organised by a consortium of schools

In some areas, there is a consortium of schools which administers one common admission test. There may also be other grammar schools in these areas which are not part of the consortium and administer their own 11+ test.

Contact the schools you're applying to to find out how the consortium works. You'll sometimes have to send an application form directly to the consortium. You will then have to apply separately to any other schools in your area which aren't part of the consortium.

Some tests are organised by individual schools

Some grammar schools have their own admissions criteria and set their own test.

Schools in these areas usually have their own Supplementary Form that you have to fill in to apply for their 11+ test. You'll need to contact each school separately to find out how to get a form and when the deadlines for applications are.

The Parents' Guide

Choosing a School

Admission rules can be complicated

The rules that schools use to allocate their places are complicated, and they can affect your child's chance of getting a place. Every school you apply to will have its own admissions policy. Familiarise yourself with each one so you know how realistic your child's chances of being offered a place are.

Some selective schools allocate places based on 'best mark first'. Children are ranked in order of their test marks, and places are offered to the children at the top of the list. However, many set an 11+ 'pass mark' then allocate places to children who score higher than this mark based on other criteria such as distance from the school and whether they have a sibling already in the school.

Many grammar schools are oversubscribed, which means that your child might not be offered a place even if they reach the 11+ pass mark. For example, if the school prioritises children who live close to the school but you live some distance away.

Fill in the Common Application Form carefully

Everyone has to fill in a secondary school application form when their child is in the autumn term of year 6. List schools in your order of preference, putting all the grammar schools first. As a back-up option, include at least one non-selective state secondary school where your child is likely to get a place. Otherwise, if your child doesn't qualify for your chosen grammar schools, the LA will allocate your child a place at any comprehensive school with unfilled places. It could be a school miles away that you really don't want. It's fine to list the non-selective school last, though.

Only writing one school on your form or writing the same school more than once will not give your child a better chance of getting a place there. List as many schools as you are able to. This gives you the most say in where your child goes to secondary school.

Independent schools may also have entrance tests

Many independent (fee-paying) schools also have their own entrance tests for entry into year 7. Some of these tests are a similar format to the 11+ tests. If you're applying to an independent school, contact them to find out more about their admissions criteria.

If you are very keen for your child to go to a selective school, it may be worth investigating an independent school as a back-up option. There are often scholarships available, and bursaries for those on a low income.

Research each school you apply to

Here's a list of things you'll need to know about the schools you apply to:

1) **How to enter for the test** — whether you have to send off any paperwork to enter your child into the test (and when the deadline for this is), or whether they'll be entered automatically.
2) **What's in the test** — what subjects will be tested (Verbal Reasoning, Maths, etc.)
3) **What's the test format** — the format the test will take (multiple choice or standard answer) and how long the test will last.
4) **Where and when the test will be**
5) **Any other admissions criteria** — e.g. distance from the school, siblings at the school, etc.
6) **Whether past papers or mock tests are available** — some schools publish past test papers or organise mock tests. They'll often charge a fee though.

The Non-Verbal Reasoning Test

Many people have never seen Non-Verbal Reasoning questions before, so it can seem daunting to explain them to a child. These pages will give you a basic introduction to Non-Verbal Reasoning.

Non-Verbal Reasoning involves shapes and diagrams

11+ Non-Verbal Reasoning questions are made up of shapes and patterns instead of words or numbers. They're designed to test your child's problem-solving and spatial reasoning skills, but they also test basic maths skills (like symmetry, adding, subtracting and dividing). Non-Verbal Reasoning is usually tested in combination with at least one other subject (Verbal Reasoning, Maths or English).

Non-Verbal Reasoning tests are designed to assess your child's intelligence and potential to succeed in grammar school, rather than how good the teaching was at their primary school. This subject is often unfamiliar to children, so it's worth familiarising your child with the types of questions they'll come across, as well as making sure they can use simple strategies to help them solve each question.

> Even if the Non-Verbal Reasoning test paper is standard answer, your child will choose an answer from some options and either write the letter, or circle it.

Non-Verbal Reasoning questions are divided into four groups

The most common Non-Verbal Reasoning questions can be divided into four groups, which test different skills:

- Similarities and Differences
- Pairs, Series and Grids
- Rotation and Reflection
- 3D Questions and Folding

For all of these question types your child will have to think about the same basic elements (see p.4-28 of the study book), so it's worth going over these first.

Similarities and Differences

The first group of questions involves finding the figure that is most like or most unlike some other figures. Question types in this group include Odd One Out, Find the Figure Like the First Two and Find the Figure Like the First Three:

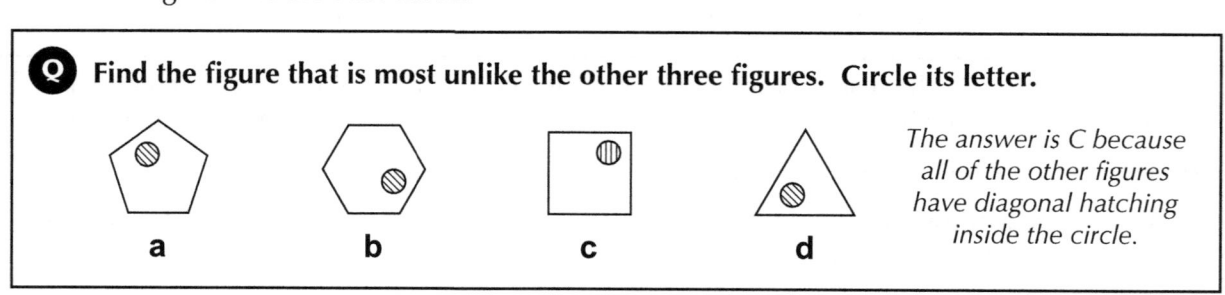

> **Q Find the figure that is most unlike the other three figures. Circle its letter.**
>
> a   b   c   d
>
> *The answer is C because all of the other figures have diagonal hatching inside the circle.*

Your child will be tested on their ability to compare different parts of the figures to spot similarities and differences. They'll need to notice small differences between figures, and consider more than one thing at a time (e.g. counting and shape), as well as spotting links between those things.

The Parents' Guide

The Non-Verbal Reasoning Test

Pairs, Series and Grids

The second group of questions involves finding the figure that completes a diagram. Question types in this group include Complete the Pair, Complete the Series and Complete the Grid:

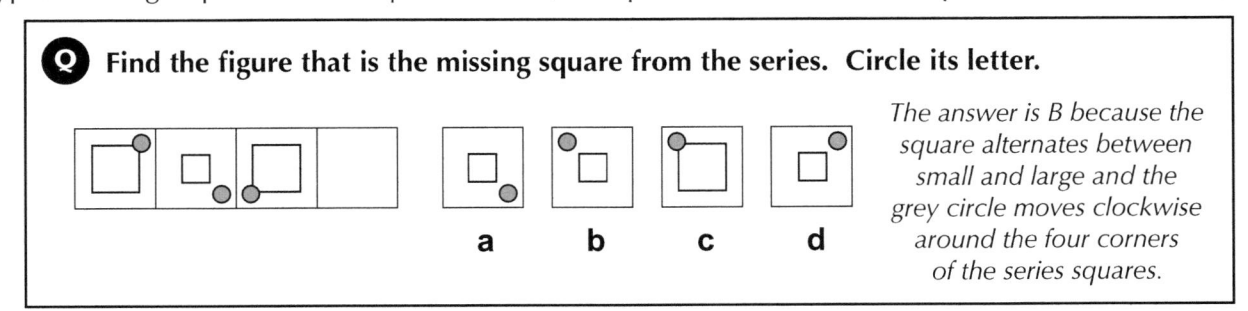

> **Q** Find the figure that is the missing square from the series. Circle its letter.
>
> *The answer is B because the square alternates between small and large and the grey circle moves clockwise around the four corners of the series squares.*

Skills that will be useful for these questions include noticing changes between figures and imagining how other figures will look if they're changed in the same way, working out how shapes will look when they're combined with other shapes, and predicting what should come next in a sequence of figures.

Rotation and Reflection

The third group of questions involves finding out how a figure will look if it is rotated or reflected. Question types in this group include Rotate the Figure and Reflect the Figure:

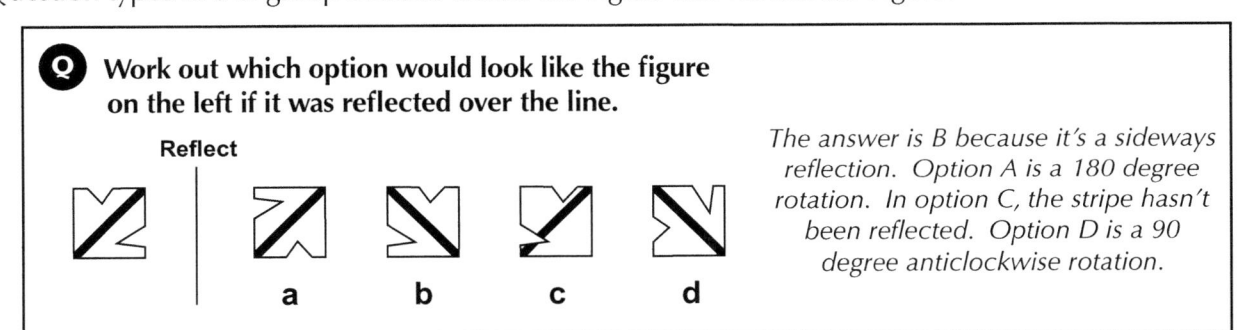

> **Q** Work out which option would look like the figure on the left if it was reflected over the line.
>
> *The answer is B because it's a sideways reflection. Option A is a 180 degree rotation. In option C, the stripe hasn't been reflected. Option D is a 90 degree anticlockwise rotation.*

To answer these questions, your child will need to be able to imagine what different figures will look like when they're reflected across a line, or rotated by different amounts (either clockwise or anticlockwise).

3D Questions and Folding

The fourth group of questions involves working with 3D shapes and with 2D shapes that are folded. Question types in this group include 3D Rotation, 3D Building Blocks, 2D Views of 3D Shapes, Cubes and Nets, Fold Along the Line and Fold and Punch:

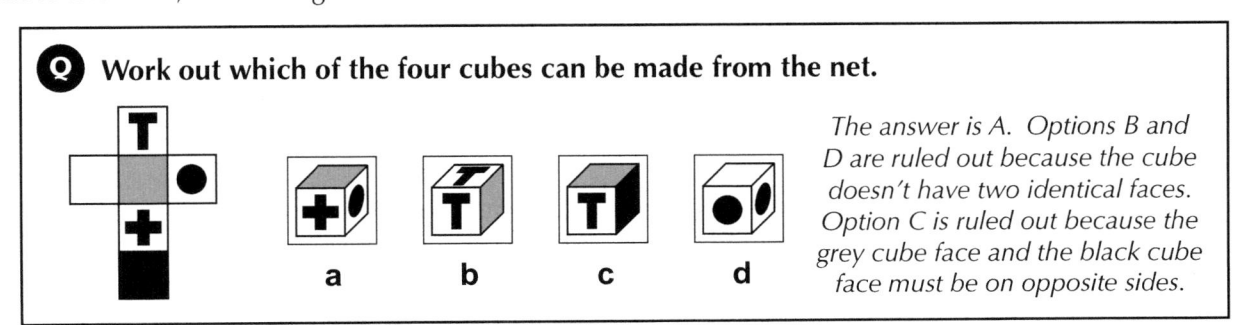

> **Q** Work out which of the four cubes can be made from the net.
>
> *The answer is A. Options B and D are ruled out because the cube doesn't have two identical faces. Option C is ruled out because the grey cube face and the black cube face must be on opposite sides.*

Questions in this group test your child's ability to rotate and combine shapes in 3D space, to imagine 3D shapes in two dimensions, to imagine 2D nets folded into 3D shapes and to imagine what a shape will look like when it is folded or unfolded.

The Parents' Guide

The Benchmark Test

You may have already decided that your child should take the 11+, or you may still be making up your mind. These pages will help you assess how far your child has to go before the test.

The benchmark test will help you assess your child

There's a pull-out benchmark test at the front of this study book. It contains 36 11+ style Non-Verbal Reasoning questions spread over three pages. The test is designed to help you find out roughly what level your child is working at, and identify their strengths and weaknesses in the Non-Verbal Reasoning part of the 11+. Each page is set at a different level — the first page is the easiest, and the questions get harder through the test.

If your child is sitting tests in other subjects as well as Non-Verbal Reasoning, you might want to test them in those subjects as well.

The benchmark test might also help you to decide whether the 11+ is right for your child — there's more information on how to assess your child's ability on page 8.

The benchmark test is in standard format

Your child should write their answer on the line on the right-hand side of the page. If their real 11+ test is in multiple choice format, don't worry — the benchmark test is just to gauge what sort of level to start your preparation at. You can practise using multiple choice answer sheets later on.

How to set the benchmark test

- Set the test at a time when your child usually works well. This might be a weekday after school, or at the weekend. This will help you get the best out of them.
- Your child should take the benchmark test at a clear table in a quiet area, free from distractions and interruptions.
- They'll need a sharp pencil, an eraser and a pencil sharpener, as well as a watch or clock so they can keep track of the time they have left.
- If your child is going to sit other benchmark tests for different subjects, don't set all the tests in the same session — if they're tired it'll affect the results of the later tests.
- Time the test strictly. Give your child 20 minutes to do as much as they can.
- Encourage them to check their answers if they finish within the time limit, but don't give them extra time to do this.
- Mark their test using the answers on the next page and use the table on page 8 to interpret their scores.

The benchmark test is designed to be as accurate as possible, but bear in mind:

- A three-page test only contains a small number of questions, so the results will never be a totally accurate prediction of the level your child is working at. It will give you a general idea though.
- The benchmark test questions are easier than the questions in the real 11+ exam, since most children will take it early on in their 11+ preparation. Even if your child scores very well on the benchmark test, this doesn't necessarily mean they're ready to take the real test.
- If your child struggles with the benchmark test and there's not much time until the 11+, it might suggest that they'll struggle with the Non-Verbal Reasoning part of the real test. See p.8 for more information on interpreting your child's results.

The Parents' Guide

The Benchmark Test

This page shows the answers to the questions in the benchmark test.
Mark the test and write your child's scores in the boxes below.

The Answers

Section One
Odd One Out
1. D   2. D   3. D   4. B

Complete the Series
5. A   6. D   7. C   8. D

Find the Figure Like the First Two
9. C   10. D   11. B   12. C   /12

Section Two
Rotate the Figure
1. C   2. B   3. A   4. C

Find the Figure Like the First Three
5. B   6. D   7. D   8. B

Complete the Pair
9. C   10. C   11. B   12. C   /12

Section Three
Odd One Out
1. C   2. E   3. C   4. D

Complete the Series
5. D   6. D   7. A   8. B

2D Views of 3D Shapes
9. B   10. A   11. B   12. D   /12

Interpreting your child's results

Add up your child's score for each section of the benchmark test and write them in the boxes above. Use the table on page 8 to interpret their results and see which level they should start working at.

The answers have been divided up by question type above. If your child struggled with questions of a particular question type, you could focus on the relevant sections of the study book.

Use the test results with information from your child's school

You can use other information to help you judge the level your child is working at. For example, you may be able to get information from their class teacher about their areas of weakness and how well they're predicted to do in their SATs. This will give you an idea of whether your child would thrive in a selective school. These schools are often highly competitive and a child who passes the 11+ can still find themselves at the bottom of the class, struggling to keep up.

NHRDE2   The Parents' Guide

Assessing Your Child

Use the test results to help you decide what to do

The benchmark test will help you work out the level to start your child's 11+ preparation. CGP's range of 11+ Non-Verbal Reasoning Practice Books are levelled from ages 7-8 to ages 10-11 (the level of the real 11+ tests). Your child's score in the benchmark test will tell you which book you should start working on.

Since this may be the first time your child has seen questions like this, the age ranges suggested by the books won't necessarily match your child's age. Don't worry if your child needs to start at the level called 'ages 7-8' when they're actually older — they should improve when they're more familiar with the questions, and they may work through the book quickly.

Add up your child's scores for each section of the test. Use the table below to find their suggested starting level. This level is only a guide — start your child at a level you think they'll be comfortable with.

Section 1	Section 2	Section 3	Where to start
9/12 or less	(This score doesn't matter.)	(This score doesn't matter.)	Non-Verbal Reasoning — CEM Ages 7-8
10/12 or more	9/12 or less	(This score doesn't matter.)	Non-Verbal Reasoning — CEM Ages 8-9
10/12 or more	10/12 or more	9/12 or less	Non-Verbal Reasoning — CEM Ages 9-10
10/12 or more	10/12 or more	10/12 or more	Non-Verbal Reasoning — CEM Ages 10-11

Have a look at the questions your child got wrong. If they were all the same question type, or the same group of question types (see p.4-5), then you could spend some extra time practising those types with your child. A lower score on the earlier pages than the later ones suggests that your child has struggled with some question types more than others.

If you only have a short time until the real test, a low score might suggest that you should spend more time focusing on Non-Verbal Reasoning questions than the other subjects your child will be tested on.

Be aware of what your child wants

Preparing for the 11+ can be a lot of work. Find out your child's opinions about the 11+, and about the schools you're applying to. Ask yourself these questions about each school:

> - Have you visited the school? Did your child like it?
> - Are all of their friends going to a different school?
> - How far is the school from your house? Will they have a long journey every day?
> - Does the school offer any extracurricular activities that your child is interested in?
> - Will your child be happy in the tough academic environment of a grammar school?

It's easy to get caught up in the routine of 11+ preparation. Remember that you can change your mind and withdraw your child from the test at any time if you decide the 11+ isn't right for them.

The Parents' Guide

Planning

These pages will help you prepare your child for their 11+ tests. They've got tips on how to plan your time, and how to help your child do their best on the day.

Make a plan

Your plan of action will depend on how much time you've got before the test. Some parents start preparing a long time in advance, but no matter how much time you have left until your child's 11+ tests, there's still plenty you can do to help them. For a lot of children, the 11+ is the first formal test they take, and it can be a stressful and daunting experience — even a small amount of preparation can boost their confidence.

Make a work plan to make sure you cover everything in time for the test.

- **Assess your child** — use the benchmark test and reports from school to assess how far you need to go before your child is fully prepared for the 11+ test (see p.6-8 for more on this).
- **Time** — ask yourself whether you and your child have enough time every week to prepare for the 11+ test. You might have to cut back on extracurricular activities or other weekly events to make time for it. Many parents find it helpful to work on the 11+ at the same time every week to fit it into their family routine.
- **Resources** — decide what resources you'll need. The Study Book will help to familiarise your child with the types of question they'll come across in the Non-Verbal Reasoning test, but you might choose to use other resources as well to help your child improve their speed and accuracy, such as practice books with assessment tests and practice test papers.

What to put in your plan

There are usually three stages of preparation for an 11+ test:

1) Learning strategies to solve each different question type.
2) Doing lots of practice of each question type (concentrating on any difficult areas and improving speed and accuracy).
3) Doing practice tests to develop test technique.

Work through the Study Book with your child. The first half of the book introduces them to the elements they will come across in Non-Verbal Reasoning questions. The second half shows them strategies to help them answer each type of question. Spend longer on the types of question that your child finds the most difficult, and work through the practice questions with them.

When your child is familiar with each topic, work through assessment papers with them to improve their speed and accuracy. Start at the level suggested by the benchmark test (see p.8) and when they're ready (when they can consistently score 85% or more), move on to the next level. Closer to the test date, start timing their work and introduce practice tests.

Keep a record of your child's 11+ scores — it'll help you to track their progress and identify areas that need more practice. It will also give your child a sense of achievement.

Remember to include the other subjects your child will be tested on in your plan. Doing a benchmark test in each subject will help you decide the best way to divide up your time.

Break up your child's work into small chunks with plenty of breaks, and introduce rewards to keep them motivated. See p.11 for more ideas on staying positive during 11+ preparation.

Preparation

Start by working on accuracy...

When your child is just learning the topics, it's a good idea to focus on accuracy and understanding, rather than speed. You can work on their speed when they're a bit more confident.

Once your child has finished a paper and you've marked it, you might want to go over the questions they got wrong, so they know how they should have solved them. You could even come back to these trickier questions at a later date to make sure they can still get them right.

Your child should aim to score over 85% in any assessment papers they do. It's a good idea to do each paper in pencil — then your child can try them again later on, to see if they can improve their score.

...then work on speed

In the real 11+ test, children are deliberately put under time pressure. This helps schools distinguish between good candidates and the best ones. The faster your child is, the more questions they'll answer. Once your child can accurately answer 11+ questions, use these tips to help them improve their speed:

- To start with, try getting them to do one question per minute in short bursts, e.g. 10 questions in 10 minutes. Gradually reduce the amount of time they have to do each question, and increase the overall time they have to spend working in one stretch (e.g. 20 questions in 15 minutes).
- Find out the timings of the real test if you can — how long your child will have, and how many questions they'll have to answer. When they're practising, give them slightly less time than this to do the same number of questions.
- Encourage your child only to check their answers if they have time at the end of the test.
- You could introduce games to get them working faster — try using a stopwatch to time each question separately, and get your child to ring a bell or shout when they've solved it.

In the run-up to the test, start working on test technique

Your child will score better on the 11+ if they improve their test technique. Good test technique is also important for their SATs, and other exams later in their education. When they start working through assessment papers, remind them to do the following things:

- Read the front of the paper and enter the correct information on it.
- Skip any questions that are really difficult, or which are taking a long time — they can come back to them if there's time at the end.
- If they can't do a question and they're running out of time, make a sensible guess.

If your child's test is in multiple choice format, there are some specific techniques to practise:

- Marking the correct box neatly and quickly using a horizontal line.
- Making sure they mark the answer in the correct box, especially if they skip a question.
- If they don't finish the paper, filling in the rest of the answers randomly.

Get your child to take some practice test papers under strict test conditions. They should work in silence and without help. Try to make their experience as close to the real test as possible.

The Parents' Guide

Motivation and Attitude

Preparation for the 11+ can take a long time, and can become quite repetitive. Your child will have school work too, so it's important to keep them motivated and positive about the 11+.

The 11+ should be a positive experience

The period leading up to the 11+ tests can be stressful, especially if you or your child feel strongly about your choice of school. If your child is spending a lot of their free time preparing for the tests, they might become tired and uncooperative. Keep a close eye on your child's behaviour and stress levels. Remember that your work plan is flexible — add breaks, games and activities into your child's study time to break up their work.

Try adding time off and rewards into your work plan. Choose small rewards to suit your child — things like sticker charts can help.

It's important to stay positive about the 11+, but be realistic about your child's chances of passing. The tests are highly competitive, and there's always a chance that they won't pass, no matter how bright they are.

There are fun things your child can do to improve

11+ practice can become a chore, so spend some time doing activities or playing games which use skills that are relevant to your child's 11+ subjects. For Non-Verbal Reasoning, these might include:

- Logic games
- Tangrams
- Jigsaw puzzles
- Spot the difference puzzles
- Match the pairs games
- Brain training games on games consoles or the internet

You could also get involved in the questions yourself — try racing your child to find the answers to individual questions, or even taking a timed paper to see if you can beat their score. You and your child could also write your own 11+ style questions, and then try to solve each other's questions.

Learn to recognise stress and to deal with it

Children react to stress in different ways, but look out for symptoms like tiredness, loss of appetite, depression, withdrawal, stomach aches or headaches. If you spot any of these signs, talk to your child and find out what's bothering them.

If they're stressed about their 11+ preparation, try adding some variety, or consider giving them a few days or a weekend off from their work. They might be stressed about other things too — year 6 can be a worrying time for children, even if they're not taking the 11+. Many schools focus heavily on SATs and the thought of secondary school can be pretty daunting.

Make sure your child keeps the test in perspective — if they're not offered a place at a selective school, it doesn't mean that they're less intelligent than other children, or that they're a failure — the 11+ only measures a few specific abilities.

Children who don't pass the 11+ test often go on to be very successful in non-selective secondary schools. Reassure your child that they can still be happy at their backup school, and that you don't measure their worth by their test scores. Encourage them not to compare themselves to other children taking the test, or to siblings who may have already gone through the 11+.

Test Day and Beyond

The test day and the time before you get the results can be just as stressful for you as for your child. Here are some tips about how to reduce this stress, and how to cope with the waiting period.

Facing the test

Make sure you and your child are fully prepared for the day of the test. You need to know:

- Where the test is and how you're going to get there (parking may be difficult).
- What time the test starts and what time you need to arrive by.
- What they'll need to bring (pencils, etc.) or whether everything is provided for them.

Make sure your child is as relaxed as possible the night before the test, and that they get a good night's sleep. Talk them through the arrangements for the test day so they know what will happen.

After the test, plan an outing or a treat which will take your child's (and your) mind off the test. Even if your child is still preparing for other 11+ tests later on in the year they'll still need a break.

- There's usually a retest day for children who are ill on the day of the test. Check with the school in advance, and let the test centre know as soon as possible if you can't make it to the test.
- If you think there are circumstances that have affected your child's performance in the test, gather evidence of this as soon as possible (e.g. a doctor's note or school marks that have dipped). Once you've got the results it'll be too late.

After the 11+

Make a plan for the time between the last of your child's tests and the day you get their results - this wait can be very stressful.

If you're going to reward your child for their hard work preparing for the 11+, you might want to do it now. If they're rewarded for their effort and hard work, they'll realise that they've achieved something, even if their results aren't what they hoped for.

This is also a good time to research the appeals process for the schools you've applied to. Some parents choose to appeal the admission decision if their child isn't offered a place (see p.13 for more on appeals).

Make sure you have a backup plan

There's a chance that your child won't score highly enough in the 11+, so have a backup plan.

Put down at least one non-selective school that your child could go to, and where they're likely to get a place (check the school's admissions criteria carefully to make sure).

If your child isn't offered a place at any of the selective schools on their Common Application Form, they will hopefully get a place at your backup, non-selective school. (If you only apply to selective schools and your child doesn't get a place, they'll be allocated a place by your LA in a school that isn't full.)

Visit your backup school as well as your preferred schools if you can, and stay as positive as possible about the possibility of your child going there. This will help if they don't get the place they want.